THE ART OF SINGING

HOW TO SING

Da Capo Press Music Reprint Series

GENERAL EDITOR

ROLAND JACKSON

UNIVERSITY OF SOUTHERN CALIFORNIA

THE ART OF SINGING

by
Luisa Tetrazzini and Enrico Caruso

HOW TO SING

by
Luisa Tetrazzini

DA CAPO PRESS · NEW YORK · 1975

Library of Congress Cataloging in Publication Data

Tetrazzini, Luisa, 1871-1940.
    The art of singing.   How to sing.

    (Da Capo Press music reprint series)
    Reprints of the 1909 ed. published by Metropolitan
Co., New York, and the 1923 ed. published by G. H. Doran
New York.
    1. Singing. I. Tetrazzini, Luisa, 1871-1940.
How to sing. 1975. II. Caruso, Enrico, 1873-1921,
joint author. III. Title. IV. Title: How to sing.
MT820.T379 1975   784.9'3   74-23417
ISBN 0-306-70674-1

This Da Capo Press edition combines in one volume the first edition of *The Art of Singing* published in New York in 1909 and *How to Sing* published in New York in 1923. Both have been published complete and unabridged.

Published by Da Capo Press, Inc.
A Subsidiary of Plenum Publishing Corporation
227 West 17th Street, New York, N.Y. 10011

The Art of Singing

By

Luisa Tetrazzini

And

Enrico Caruso

NEW YORK
THE METROPOLITAN COMPANY, *Publishers*
25 West Forty-second Street
1909

Printed by William Green, New York

IN OFFERING this work to the public the publishers wish to lay before those who sing or who are about to study singing, the simple, fundamental rules of the art based on common sense. The two greatest living exponents of the art of singing—Luisa Tetrazzini and Enrico Caruso—have been chosen as examples, and their talks on singing have additional weight from the fact that what they have to say has been printed exactly as it was uttered, the truths they expound are driven home forcefully, and what they relate so simply is backed by years of experience and emphasized by the results they have achieved as the two greatest artists in the world.

Much has been said about the Italian Method of Singing. It is a question whether anyone really knows what the phrase means. After all, if there be a right way to sing, then all other ways must be wrong. Books have been written on breathing, tone production and what singers should eat and wear, etc., etc., all tending to make the singer self-conscious and to sing with the brain rather than with the heart. To quote Mme. Tetrazzini: "You can train the voice, you can take a raw material and make it a finished production; not so with the heart."

The country is overrun with inferior teachers of singing; men and women who have failed to get before the public, turn to teaching without any practical experience, and, armed only with a few methods, teach these alike to all pupils, ruining many good voices. Should these pupils change teachers, even for the better, then begins the weary undoing of the false method, often with no better result.

To these unfortunate pupils this book is of inestimable value. He or she could not consistently choose such teachers after reading its pages. Again the simple rules laid down and tersely and interestingly set forth not only carry conviction with them, but tear away the veil of mystery that so often is thrown about the divine art.

Luisa Tetrazzini and Enrico Caruso show what not to do, as well as what to do, and bring the pupil back to first principles—the art of singing naturally.

LUISA TETRAZZINI

LUISA TETRAZZINI

L UISA TETRAZZINI, the most famous Italian
coloratura soprano of the day, declares that she
began to sing before she learned to talk. Her
parents were not musical, but her elder sister, now
the wife of the eminent conductor Cleofante Campanini, was a public singer of established reputation,
and her success roused her young sister's ambition to
become a great artist. Her parents were well to do,
her father having a large army furnishing store in
Florence, and they did not encourage her in her determination to become a prima donna. One prima donna,
said her father, was enough for any family.

Luisa did not agree with him. If one prima donna is
good, she argued, why would not two be better? So
she never desisted from her importunity until she was
permitted to become a pupil of Professor Coccherani,
vocal instructor at the Lycée. At this time she had
committed to memory more than a dozen grand opera
rôles, and at the end of six months the professor con-
fessed that he could do nothing more for her voice; that
she was ready for a career.

She made her bow to the Florentine opera going
public, one of the most critical in Italy, as Inez, in
Meyerbeer's "L'Africaine," and her success was so
pronounced that she was engaged at a salary of $100 a
month, a phenomenal beginning for a young singer.
Queen Margherita was present on the occasion and com-

plimented her highly and prophesied for her a great career. She asked the trembling débutante how old she was, and in the embarrassment of the moment Luisa made herself six years older than she really was. This is one noteworthy instance in which a public singer failed to discount her age.

Fame came speedily, but for a long time it was confined to Europe and Latin America. She sang seven seasons in St. Petersburg, three in Mexico, two in Madrid, four in Buenos Aires, and even on the Pacific coast of America before she appeared in New York. She had sung Lucia more than 200 times before her first appearance at Covent Garden, and the twenty curtain calls she received on that occasion came as the greatest surprise of her career. She had begun to believe that she could never be appreciated by English-speaking audiences and the ovation almost overcame her.

It was by the merest chance that Mme. Tetrazzini ever came to the Manhattan Opera House in New York. The diva's own account of her engagement is as follows:

"I was in London, and for a wonder I had a week, a wet week, on my hands. You know people will do anything in a wet week in London.

"There were contracts from all over the Continent and South America pending. There was much discussion naturally in regard to settlements and arrangements of one kind and another.

"Suddenly, just like that"—she makes a butterfly gesture—"M. Hammerstein came, and just like that"—a duplicate gesture—"I made up my mind that I would come here. If his offer to me had been seven days later I should not have signed, and if I had not I should undoubtedly never have come, for a contract that I might have signed to go elsewhere would probably have been for a number of years."

Voice experts confess that they are not able to solve the mystery of Mme. Tetrazzini's wonderful management of her breathing.

"It is perfectly natural," she says. "I breathe low down in the diaphragm, not, as some do, high up in the upper part of the chest. I always hold some breath in reserve for the crescendos, employing only what is absolutely necessary, and I renew the breath wherever it is easiest.

"In breathing I find, as in other matters pertaining to singing, that as one goes on and practices, no matter how long one may have been singing, there are constantly new surprises awaiting one. You may have been accustomed for years to take a note in a certain way, and after a long while you discover that, while it is a very good way, there is a better."

****
Breath Control
The Foundation of Singing
****

THERE is only one way to sing correctly, and that is to sing naturally, easily, comfortably.

The height of vocal art is to have no apparent method, but to be able to sing with perfect facility from one end of the voice to the other, emitting all the notes clearly and yet with power and having each note of the scale sound the same in quality and tonal beauty as the ones before and after.

There are many methods which lead to the goal of natural singing—that is to say, the production of the voice with ease, beauty and with perfect control.

Some of the greatest teachers in the world reach this point apparently by diverging roads.

Around the art of singing there has been formed a cult which includes an entire jargon of words meaning one thing to the singer and another thing to the rest of the world and which very often doesn't mean the same thing to two singers of different schools.

In these talks with you I am going to try to use the simplest words, and the few idioms which I will have to take from my own language I will translate to you as clearly as I can, so that there can be no misunderstanding.

Certainly the highest art and a lifetime of work and study are necessary to acquire an easy emission of tone.

There are quantities of wonderful natural voices, particularly among the young people of Switzerland and Italy, and the American voice is especially noted for its purity and the beauty of its tone in the high registers.

But these naturally untrained voices soon break or fail if they are used much unless the singer supplements the natural, God-given vocal gifts with a conscious understanding of how the vocal apparatus should be used.

The singer must have some knowledge of his or her anatomical structure, particularly the structure of the throat, mouth and face, with its resonant cavities, which are so necessary for the right production of the voice.

Besides that, the lungs and diaphragm and the whole breathing apparatus must be understood, because the foundation of singing is breathing and breath control.

A singer must be able to rely on his breath, just as he relies upon the solidity of the ground beneath his feet.

A shaky, uncontrolled breath is like a rickety foundation on which nothing can be built, and until that foundation has been developed and strengthened the would-be singer need expect no satisfactory results.

From the girls to whom I am talking especially I must now ask a sacrifice—the singer cannot wear tight corsets and should not wear corsets of any kind which come up higher than the lowest rib.

In other words, the corset must be nothing but a belt, but with as much hip length as the wearer finds convenient and necessary.

In order to insure proper breathing capacity it is understood that the clothing must be absolutely loose around the chest and also across the lower part of the back, for one should breathe with the back of the lungs as well as with the front.

In my years of study and work I have developed my own breathing capacity until I am somewhat the despair of the fashionable modiste, but I have a diaphragm and a breath on which I can rely at all times.

In learning to breathe it is well to think of the lungs

as empty sacks, into which the air is dropping like a weight, so that you think first of filling the bottom of your lungs, then the middle part, and so on until no more air can be inhaled.

Inhale short breaths through the nose. This. of course, is only an exercise for breath development.

Now begin to inhale from the bottom of the lungs first.

Exhale slowly and feel as if you were pushing the air against your chest. If you can get this sensation later when singing it will help you very greatly to get control of the breath and to avoid sending too much breath through the vocal chords.

The breath must be sent out in an even, steady flow.

You will notice when you begin to sing, if you watch yourself very carefully, that, first, you will try to inhale too much air; secondly, you will either force it all out at once, making a breathy note, or in trying to control the flow of air by the diaphragm you will suddenly cease to send it forth at all and will be making the sound by pressure from the throat.

There must never be any pressure from the throat. The sound must be made from the continued flow of air.

You must learn to control this flow of air, so that no muscular action of the throat can shut it off.

Open the throat wide and start your note by the pressure breath. The physical sensation should be first an effort on the part of the diaphragm to press the air up against the chest box, then the sensation of a perfectly open throat, and, lastly, the sensation that the air is passing freely into the cavities of the head.

The quantity of sound is controlled by the breath.

In diminishing the tone the opening of the throat remains the same. Only the quantity of breath given forth is diminished.   That is done by the diaphragm muscles.

"Filare la voce," to spin the voice from a tiny little thread into a breadth of sound and then diminish again, is one of the most beautiful effects in singing.

It is accomplished by the control of the breath, and its perfect accomplishment means the complete mastery of the greatest difficulty in learning to sing.

I think one of the best exercises for learning to control the voice by first getting control of the breath is to stand erect in a well-ventilated room or out of doors and slowly snuff in air through the nostrils, inhaling in little puffs, as if you were smelling something.

Take just a little bit of air at a time and feel as if you were filling the very bottom of your lungs and also the back of your lungs.

When you have the sensation of being full up to the neck retain the air for a few seconds and then very slowly send it out in little puffs again.

This is a splendid exercise, but I want to warn you not to practise any breathing exercise to such an extent that you make your heart beat fast or feel like strangling.

Overexercising the lungs is as bad as not exercising them enough and the results are often harmful.

Like everything else in singing, you want to learn this gradually.   Never neglect it, because it is the very foundation of your art.   But don't try to develop a diaphragm expansion of five inches in two weeks.

Indeed, it is not the expansion that you are working for.

I have noticed this one peculiarity about young singers—if they have an enormous development of the diaphragm they think they should be able to sing, no matter what happens. A girl came to see me once whose figure was really entirely out of proportion, the lower part of the lungs having been pressed out quite beyond even artistic lines.

"You see, madam," she exclaimed, "I have studied breathing. Why, I have such a strong diaphragm I can move the piano with it!" And she did go right up to my piano and, pushing on this strong diaphragm of hers, moved the piano a fraction of an inch from its place.

I was quite aghast. I had never met such an athletic singer. When I asked her to let me hear her voice, however, a tiny stream of contralto sound issued from those powerful lungs.

She had developed her breathing capacity, but when she sang she held her breath back.

I have noticed that a great many people do this, and it is one of the things that must be overcome in the very beginning of the study of singing.

Certain young singers take in an enormous breath, stiffening every muscle in order to hold the air, thus depriving their muscles of all elasticity.

They will then shut off the throat and let only the smallest fraction of air escape, just enough to make a sound. Too much inbreathing and too violent an effort at inhaling will not help the singer at all.

People have said that they cannot see when I breathe. Well, they certainly cannot say that I am ever short of breath even if I do try to breathe invisibly. When I breathe I scarcely draw my diaphragm in at all, but I feel the air fill my lungs and I feel my upper ribs expand.

In singing I always feel as if I were forcing my breath against my chest, and, just as in the exercises accord-

ing to Delsarte you will find the chest leads in all physical movements, so in singing you should feel this firm
support of the chest of the highest as well as the lowest
notes.

I have seen pupils, trying to master the art of
breathing, holding themselves as rigidly as drum
majors.

Now this rigidity of the spinal column will in no
way help you in the emission of tone, nor will it increase
the breath control. In fact, I don't think it would
even help you to stand up straight, although it would
certainly give one a stiff appearance and one far removed from grace.

A singer should stand freely and easily and should
feel as if the chest were leading, but should not feel con-
strained or stiff in any part of the ribs or lungs.

From the minute the singer starts to emit a tone the
supply of breath must be emitted steadily from the
chamber of air in the lungs. It must never be held
back once.

The immediate pressure of the air should be felt more
against the chest. I know of a great many singers who,
when they come to very difficult passages, put their
hands on their chests, focusing their attention on this
one part of the mechanism of singing.

The audience, of course, thinks the prima donna's
hand is raised to her heart, when, as a matter of fact,
the prima donna, with a difficult bit of singing before
her, is thinking of her technique and the foundation of
that technique—breath control.

This feeling of singing against the chest with the
weight of air pressing up against it is known as "breath
support," and in Italian we have even a better word,
"apoggio," which is breath prop. The diaphragm in

English may be called the bellows of the lungs, but the apoggio is the deep breath regulated by the diaphragm.

The attack of the sound must come from the apoggio, or breath prop. In attacking the very highest notes it is essential, and no singer can really get the high notes or vocal flexibility or strength of tone without the attack coming from this seat of respiration.

In practising the trill or staccato tones the pressure of the breath must be felt even before the sound is heard. The beautiful, clear, bell-like tones that die away into a soft piano are tones struck on the apoggio and controlled by the steady soft pressure of the breath emitted through a perfectly open throat, over a low tongue and resounding in the cavities of the mouth or head.

Never for a moment sing without this apoggio, this breath prop. Its development and its constant use mean the restoration of sick or fatigued voices and the prolonging of all one's vocal powers into what is wrongly called old age.

The Mastery of the Tongue

THE tongue is a veritable stumbling block in the path of the singer. The tongue is an enormous muscle compared with the other parts of the throat and mouth, and its roots particularly can by a slight movement block the passage of the throat pressing against the larynx. This accounts for much of the pinched singing we hear.

When the tongue forms a mountain in the back part of the mouth the singer produces what you call in English slang "a hot potato tone"—that is to say, a tone that sounds as if it were having much difficulty to get through the mouth. In very fact, it is having this difficulty, for it has to pass over the back of the tongue.

The would-be singer has to learn to control the tongue muscles and, above all things, to learn to relax the tongue and to govern it at will, so that it never stiffens and forms that hard lump which can be plainly felt immediately beneath the chin under the jaw.

It requires a great deal of practice to gain control of the tongue, and there are many different exercises which purport to be beneficial in gaining complete mastery over it. One, for instance, is to throw the tongue out as far forward as possible without stiffening it and then draw it back slowly. This can be done in front of a mirror by trying to throw the tongue not only from the tip, but from the root, keeping the sides of the tongue broad. Another way is to catch hold of the two sides of the tongue with the fingers and pull it out gently.

17

For my part, I scarcely approve of these mechanical ways of gaining control of the tongue except in cases where the singer is phlegmatic of temperament and cannot be made to feel the various sensations of stiff tongue or tongue drawn far back in other ways. Ordinarily I think they make the singer conscious, nervous and more likely to stiffen the tongue in a wild desire to relax it and keep it flat.

These exercises, however, combined with exercises in diction, help to make the tongue elastic, and the more elastic and quick this muscle becomes the clearer will be the singer's diction and the more flexible will be her voice.

The correct position of the tongue is raised from the back, lying flat in the mouth, the flattened tip beneath the front teeth, with the sides slightly raised so as to form a slight furrow in it. When the tongue is lying too low a lump under the chin beneath the jaw will form in singing and the tight muscles can be easily felt.

When the jaw is perfectly relaxed and the tongue lies flat in the mouth there will be a slight hollow under the chin and no stiffness in the muscles.

The tip of the tongue of course is employed in the pronunciation of the consonants and must be so agile that the minute it has finished its work it at once resumes the correct position.

In ascending the scale the furrow in the tongue increases as we come to the higher notes. It is here that the back of the palate begins to draw up in order to add to the resonance of the head notes, giving the cavities of the head free play.

You can easily see your back palate working by opening your mouth wide and giving yourself the

sensation of one about to sneeze. You will see far
back in the throat, way behind the nose, a soft spot
that will draw up of itself as the sneeze becomes more
imminent. That little point is the soft palate. It
must be drawn up for the high notes in order to get
the head resonance. As a singer advances in her art
she can do this at will.

The adjustment of throat, tongue and palate, all
working together, will daily respond more easily to
her demands. However, she should be able consciously
to control each part by itself.

The conscious direction of the voice and command
of the throat are necessary. Frequently in opera
the singer, sitting or lying in some uncomfortable
position which is not naturally convenient for producing the voice, will consciously direct her notes
into the head cavities by opening up the throat and
lifting the soft palate. For instance, in the role of
Violetta the music of the last act is sung lying down.
In order to get proper resonance to some of the high
notes I have to start them in the head cavity by means,
of course, of the apoggio, or breath prop, without
which the note would be thin and would have no
body to it.

The sensation that I have is of a slight pressure of
breath striking almost into a direct line into the
cavity behind the forehead over the eyes without
any obstruction or feeling in the throat at all.

This is the correct attack for the head tone, or a
tone taken in the upper register. Before I explain
the registers to you I must tell you one of the funniest
compliments I ever received. A very flattering person
was comparing my voice to that of another high
soprano whom I very much admire.

"Her voice is beautiful, particularly in the upper register," I insisted when the other lady was being criticized.

"Ah, madame," responded the flattering critic, "but your registers give out so much more warmth."

I think this joke is too good to lose, also the criticism, while unjust to the other singer, is interesting to the student, because in the high register, which includes in some voices all the notes above middle C, the notes are thin and cold unless supported by the apoggio, the breath prop, of which I have told you so much. People ask whether there are such things as vocal registers. Certainly there are. There are three always and sometimes four in very high voices. The ordinary registers are the low, the middle, the high voice, or head voice, and sometimes the second high voice, which has been called the flagellant voice.

A vocal register is a series of tones which are produced by a certain position of the larynx, tongue and palate. In the woman's voice the middle register takes in the notes from E on the first line of the staff about to middle C. The head voice begins at middle C and runs up sometimes to the end of the voice, sometimes to B flat or C, where it joins the second head register, which I have heard ascend into a whistle in phenomenal voices cultivated only in this register and useless for vocal work.

Though the registers exist and the tones in middle, below and above are not produced in the same manner, the voice should be so equalized that the change in registers cannot be heard. And a tone sung with a head voice and in the low voice should have the same degree of quality, resonance and power.

As the voice ascends in the scale each note is different, and as one goes on up the positions of the organ of the throat cannot remain the same for several different tones. But there should never be an abrupt change, either audible to the audience or felt in the singer's throat. Every tone must be imperceptibly prepared, and upon the elasticity of the vocal organs depends the smoothness of the tone production. Adjusting the vocal apparatus to the high register should be both imperceptible and mechanical whenever a high note has to be sung.

In the high register the head voice, or voice which vibrates in the head cavities, should be used chiefly. The middle register requires palatal resonance, and the first notes of the head register and the last ones of the middle require a judicious blending of both. The middle register can be dragged up to the high notes, but always at the cost first of the beauty of the voice and then of the voice itself, for no organ can stand being used wrongly for a long time.

This is only one of the reasons that so many fine big voices go to pieces long before they should.

In an excess of enthusiasm the young singer attempts to develop the high notes and make them sound—in her own ears, at all events—as big as the middle voice. The pure head tone sounds small and feeble to the singer herself, and she would rather use the chest quality, but the head tone has the piercing, penetrating quality which makes it tell in a big hall, while the middle register, unless used in its right place, makes the voice muffled, heavy and lacking in vibrancy. Though to the singer the tone may seem immense, in reality it lacks resonance.

A singer must never cease listening to herself intelligently and never neglect cultivating the head tone or over-tone of the voice, which is its salvation, for it means vibrancy, carrying power and youth to a voice. Without it the finest voice soon becomes worn and off pitch. Used judiciously it will preserve a voice into old age.

Tone Emission and Attack

IN my first talk I said a few words, but not half enough, on the subject of breath control.

My second talk was the physiological aspect of the throat, head and tongue, for it is necessary to become thoroughly acquainted with the mechanism with which you are to work before you can really sing. Today I'm going to take up the subject of tone emission and the attack.

A great many singers suffer from the defect called "throatiness" of the emission—that is to say, they attack or start the note in the throat. Sooner or later this attack will ruin the most beautiful voice. As I have said before, the attack of the note must come from the apoggio, or breath prop. But to have the attack pure and perfectly in tune you must have the throat entirely open, for it is useless to try to sing if the throat is not sufficiently open to let the sound pass freely. Throaty tones or pinched tones are tones which are trying to force themselves through a half-closed throat blocked either by insufficient opening of the larynx or by stoppage of the throat passage, due to the root of the tongue being forced down and back too hard or possibly to a low, soft palate.

In order to have the throat perfectly open it is necessary to have the jaw absolutely relaxed.

I have found in studying different nationalities that it is fairly easy for the French and Spanish people to learn this relaxation of jaw and the opening of the throat, but the English-speaking people generally talk with the throat half shut and even talk through half-

shut teeth.   Sometime, when you are talking rapidly,
suddenly put your hand up to your jaw.   You will find
that it is stiff; that the muscles beneath it (tongue
muscles) are tight and hard; that the jaw seldom goes
down very far in pronouncing any of the English words,
whereas in singing the jaw should be absolutely relaxed,
going down and back just as far as it can with ease.

The jaw is attached to the skull right beneath the
temples in front of the ears.   By placing your two
fingers there and dropping the jaw you will find that a
space between the skull and jaw grows as the jaw drops.

In singing this space must be as wide as is possible,
for that indicates that the jaw is dropped down, giving
its aid to the opening at the back of the throat.   It will
help the beginner sometimes to do simple relaxing exercises, feeling the jaw drop with the fingers.   It must
drop down, and it is not necessary to open the mouth
wide, because the jaw is relaxed to its utmost.

However, for a beginner it is as well to practice
opening the mouth wide, being sure to lower the jaw at
the back.   Do this many times a day without emitting
any sound merely to get the feeling of what an open
throat is really like.   You will presently begin to yawn
after you have done the exercise a couple of times.   In
yawning or in starting to drink a sip of water the throat
is widely open, and the sensation is a correct one which
the singer must study to reproduce.

I have noticed a great many actors and actresses in
America who speak with jaws tightly closed, or at least
closed to such an extent that only the smallest emission
of breath is possible.   Such a voice production will
never allow the actor to express any varying degree of
emotion and will also completely eradicate any natural
beauty of tone which the voice may have.   However,

this is a fault which can easily be overcome by practicing this daily relaxation of the jaw and always when singing breathing as if the jaw hung perfectly loose, or, better still, as if you had none at all.   When you can see a vocalist pushing on the jaw you can be perfectly certain that the tone she is emitting at that moment is a forced note and that the whole vocal apparatus is being tortured to create what is probably not a pleasant noise.

Any kind of mental distress will cause the jaw to stiffen and will have an immediate effect upon the voice. This is one of the reasons why a singer must learn to control her emotions and must not subject herself to any harrowing experiences, even such as watching a sensational spectacle, before she is going to sing. Fear, worry, fright—stage as well as other kinds—set the jaw. So does too great a determination to succeed. A singer's mind must control all of her feelings if it is going to control her voice. She must be able even to surmount a feeling of illness or stage fright and to control her vocal apparatus, as well as her breath, no matter what happens.

The singer should feel as if her jaw were detached and falling away from her face. As one great singer expresses it: "You should have the jaw of an imbecile when emitting a tone. In fact, you shouldn't know that you have one." Let us take the following passage from "The Marriage of Figaro," by Mozart:

Voi-che sa-pe-te-

This would make an excellent exercise for the jaw. Sing only the vowels, dropping the jaw as each one is attacked—"o, eh, ah." The o, of course, is pronounced

like the English o and the i in voi like e.   The e in che
is pronounced like the English a.   Sapete is pronounced
sahpata.   You now have the vowels, o, ee, a, ah, a.
Open the throat wide, drop the jaw and pronounce
the tones on a note in the easiest part of your voice.

Do not attack a note at the same time that you are
inhaling.   That is too soon.   Take the breath through
the nose, of course, and give it an instant to settle before
attacking the sound.   In this way you will avoid the
stroke of the glottis which is caused by the sudden and
uncontrolled emission of the accumulated breath.   In
attacking a note the breath must be directed to the
focusing point on the palate which lies just at the
critical spot, different for every tone.   In attacking a
note, however, there must be no pressure on this place,
because if there is the overtones will be unable to soar
and sound with the tone.

From the moment the note is attacked the breath
must flow out with it.   It is a good idea to feel at first
as if one were puffing out the breath.   This is particularly good for the high notes on which a special stress
must be laid always to attack with the breath and not
to press or push with the throat.   As long as the tone
lasts the gentle but uninterrupted outpouring of the
breath must continue behind it.   This breath pressure
insures the strength and, while holding the note to the
focusing point on the palate, insures its pitch.   In a
general way it can be said that the medium tones of the
voice have their focusing point in the middle part of the
palate, the lower tones coming nearer to the teeth to be
centralized and the high notes giving the sensation of
finding their focusing point in the high arch at the back
of the mouth and going out, as it were, through the
crown of the head.

The resonance in the head cavities is soon perceived by those who are beginning to sing. Sometimes in producing their first high notes young people become nervous and irritated when singing high tones at the curious buzzing in the head and ears. After a short time, however, this sensation is no longer an irritation, and the singer can gauge in a way where his tones are placed by getting a mental idea of where the resonance to each particular tone should be.

High notes with plenty of head vibration can only be obtained when the head is clear and the nasal cavities unobstructed by mucous membrane or by any of the depression which comes from physical or mental cause. The best way to lose such depression is to practice. Practicing the long scale, being careful to use the different registers, as described later, will almost invariably even out the voice and clear out the head if continued long enough, and will enable the singer to overcome nervous or mental depression as well.

The different sensations in producing the tone vary according to the comparative height and depth. Beginning from the medium tones, the singer will feel as if each tone of the descending scale were being sung farther outside of the mouth, the vibration hitting the upper teeth as it goes out, whereas with the ascending scale the vibrations pass through the nasal cavities, through the cavity in the forehead and up back into the head, until one feels as if the tone were being formed high over the head at the back.

I want to say right here that whenever a young singer feels uncomfortable when singing he or she is singing incorrectly.

In attacking the note on the breath, particularly in the high notes, it is quite possible that at first the voice will not respond.   For a long time merely an emission or breath or perhaps a little squeak on the high note is all that can be hoped for.   If, however, this is continued, eventually the head voice will be joined to the breath, and a faint note will find utterance which with practice will develop until it becomes an easy and brilliant tone.

The reason that the tone has not been able to come forth is because the vocal apparatus cannot adjust itself to the needs of the vocal chords or because they themselves have not accustomed themselves to respond to the will of the singer and are too stiff to perform their duty.

The scale is the greatest test of voice production. No opera singer, no concert singer, who cannot sing a perfect scale can be said to be a technician or to have achieved results in her art.   Whether the voice be soprano, mezzo or contralto, each note should be perfect of its kind, and the note of each register should partake sufficiently of the quality of the next register above or below it in order not to make the transition noticeable when the voice ascends or descends the scale.   This blending of the registers is obtained by the intelligence of the singer in mixing the different tone qualities of the registers, using as aids the various formations of the lips, mouth and throat and the ever present apoggic without which no perfect scale can be sung.

IN studying a new rôle I am in the habit of practicing in front of a mirror in order to get an idea of the effect of a facial expression and to see that it does not take away from the correct position of the mouth.

The young singer should practice constantly in front of a mirror as soon as she begins to sing songs or to express emotions in her music, for the girl with the expressive face is likely to contort her mouth so that the correct emission of tones is impossible.

The dramatic artist depends largely for her expression on the changing lines of the mouth, chin and jaw, and in any lines spoken which denote command or will you will see the actor's jaw setting and becoming rigid with the rest of the facial mask.

Now, a singer can never allow the facial expression to alter the position of the jaw or mouth. Facial expression for the singer must concern itself chiefly with the eyes and forehead.

The mouth must remain the same, and the jaw must ever be relaxed, whether the song is one of deep intensity or a merry scale of laughter.

The mouth in singing should always smile lightly. This slight smile at once relaxes the lips, allowing them free play for the words which they and the tongue must form and also gives the singer a slight sensation of uplift necessary for singing.

It is impossible to sing well when mentally depressed or even physically indisposed slightly. Unless one has complete control over the entire vocal apparatus and unless one can simulate a smile one does not feel the

29

voice will lack some of its resonant quality, particularly in the upper notes, where the smiling position of the mouth adjusts the throat and air passages for the emission of light tones.

The lips are of the greatest aid in shaping and shading the tones. Wagnerian singers, for instance, who employ trumpet-like notes in certain passages are often seen shaping their lips like the mouthpiece of a trumpet, with a somewhat square opening, the lips protruding.

However, this can be practiced only after perfect relaxation of the jaw and control of the tongue have been accomplished.

A singer's mouth must always look pleasant, not only because it creates a disagreeable impression on the audience to see a crooked and contorted mouth, but also because natural and correct voice production requires a mouth shaped almost into a smile.

Too wide a smile often accompanies what is called "the white voice." This is a voice production where a head resonance alone is employed, without sufficient of the apoggio or enough of the mouth resonance to give the tone a vital quality. This "white voice" should be thoroughly understood and is one of the many shades of tone a singer can use at times, just as the impressionist uses various unusual colors to produce certain atmospheric effects.

For instance, in the mad scene in "Lucia" the use of the "white voice" suggests the babbling of the mad woman, as the same voice in the last act of "Traviata" or in the last act of "Bohemè" suggests utter physical exhaustion and the approach of death.

An entire voice production on these colorless lines, however, would always lack the brilliancy and the vitality which inspire enthusiasm.

One of the compensations of the "white voice" singer is the fact that she usually possesses a perfect diction. The voice itself is thrust into the head cavities and not allowed to vibrate in the face and mouth and gives ample room for the formation of vowels and consonants. And the singer with this voice production usually concentrates her entire attention on diction.

The cure for this tone emission is, first of all, the cultivation of the breath prop, then attacking the vowel sound o o in the medium voice, which requires a low position of the larynx, and exercises on the ascending scale until the higher notes have been brought down, as it were, and gain some of the body and support of the lower notes without losing their quality.

The singer's expression must concern itself chiefly with the play of emotion around the eyes, eyebrows and forehead. You have no idea how much expression you can get out of your eyebrows, for instance, until you study the question and learn by experiment that a complete emotional scale can be symbolized outwardly in the movements of the eyelids and eyebrows.

A very drooping eyebrow is expressive of fatigue, either physical or mental. This lowered eyelid is the aspect we see about us most of the time, particularly on people past their first youth. As it shows a lack of interest, it is not a favorite expression of actors and is only employed where the rôle makes it necessary.

Increasing anxiety is depicted by slanting the eyebrows obliquely in a downward line toward the nose.

Concentrated attention draws the eyebrows together over the bridge of the nose, while furtiveness widens the space again without elevating the eyebrows.

In the eyebrows alone you can depict mockery, every

stage of anxiety or pain, astonishment, ecstasy, terror, suffering, fury and admiration, besides all the subtle tones between.

In singing rôles of songs it is necessary to practice before the mirror in order to see that this facial expression is present and that it is not exaggerated; that the face is not contorted by lines of suffering or by the lines of mirth.

Another thing the young singer must not forget in making her initial bow before the public is the question of dress. When singing on the platform or stage, dress as well as you can. Whenever you face the public have at least the assurance you are looking your very best; that your gowns hang well, are well fitted and are of a becoming color.

It is not necessary that they should be gorgeous or expensive, but let them always be suitable, and for big cities let them be just as sumptuous as you can afford. At morning concerts in New York, velvets and hand-painted chiffons are considered good form, while in the afternoon handsome silk or satin frocks of a very light color are worn with hats.

If a singer chooses to wear a hat let her be sure that its shape will not interfere with her voice.

A very large hat, for instance, with a wide brim that comes down over the face, acts as a sort of blanket to the voice, eating up the sound and detracting from the beauty of tone, which should go forth into the audience. It is also likely to shade the singer's features too much and hide her from view from those sitting in the balconies or galleries. As a rule, the singer's hat should be small or with a flaring brim, which does not detract from the tone.

Another word on the subject of corsets. There is

no reason in the world why a singer should not wear corsets, and if singers have a tendency to grow stout a corset is usually a necessity. A singer's corset should be especially well fitted around the hips and should be extremely loose over the diaphragm.

If made in this way it will not interfere in the slightest degree with the breath.

Now as to diet and the general mode of life. Every singer must take care of her health. But that does not necessarily mean that she must wrap herself in cotton batting and lead a sequestered existence. I don't believe that any person who wants to make a public career can accomplish it and also indulge in social dissipations. Society must be cut out of the life of the would-be singer, for the demands made by it on time and vitality can only be given at a sacrifice to one's art.

The care of the health is an individual matter, and what agrees well with me would cause others to sicken. I eat the simplest food always, and naturally, being an Italian, I prefer the food of my native land. But simple French or German cookery agrees with me quite as well. And I allow the tempting pastry, the rich and overspiced pâté, to pass me by untouched and console myself with quantities of fruit and fresh vegetables.

Personally I never wear a collar and have hardened my throat to a considerable extent by wearing slightly cutout gowns always in the house, and even when I wear furs I do not have them closely drawn around the neck. I try to keep myself at an even bodily temperature, and fresh air has been my most potent remedy at all times when I have been indisposed.

THERE is nothing so beneficial to the young artist as the kindly and just criticism of a person who knows and nothing so stimulating as his praise.

Among my most priceless possessions I treasure the words of encouragement given me by Patti and Sembrich, those wonderful artists, when I was beginning my career.

Mme. Patti is a splendid example of the many sidedness necessary to artistic perfection. Her wonderful voice was always supplemented by complete knowledge of the art of singing, and her mastery of languages and of different fields of art made her not only a great artist, but a most interesting woman.

To hear an artist of this kind is one of the most profitable parts of a musical education.

But there are two ways of listening to a singer. There is the appreciative way, and there is the entirely critical. The beginner usually tries to show her knowledge by her intensely critical attitude.

The older you become in your art the more readily you will be able to appreciate and learn from the singers you hear on the opera or concert stage.

The greatest and the humblest singer can teach you something. But to learn you must be in a receptive attitude.

The public has no real conception of what an amount of intelligent work besides talent and art is necessary to achieve the results which it sees or hears. Only those whose lives are devoted to the same ideals can

understand the struggles of other artists, and it is for
that reason that appreciation and not condemnation
should be on the tongues of those who themselves
have studied.

The artist may demand the greatest things of
herself, and what may be good enough for others
is not good enough for her. As the poet says, "Art
is long," though life may be short, and singing is one
of the most fleeting of all arts, since once the note is
uttered it leaves only a memory in the hearer's mind
and since so many beautiful voices, for one reason or
other, go to pieces long before their time.

If the singer's health is good the voice should end
only with life itself, provided, of course, it has been
used with understanding and with art.

In performing before the public one should be
governed by the tastes of the public, not by one's
own tastes. Just as the comedian usually wishes to
play Hamlet and the man of tragic mien thinks he
could be a comedy star, the singer who could make
a fortune at interpreting chansonnettes usually wishes
to sing operatic roles, and the singer with a deep
and heavy voice is longing to inflict baby songs on a
long suffering public.

It is easy enough to find out what the public wishes
to hear, and, though one should always be enlarging
one's repertory, it is not a bad idea to stick to that
field for which one is particularly fitted vocally and
physically.

In studying a rôle after one has mastered the technical difficulties one should try to steep one's personality into that of the character one is to portray, and
for that reason all study, no matter what it is, and
reading of all kinds help one in developing a part.

The great Italian tragedienne, Duse, told me that one of her greatest pleasures was to wander about the streets incognito watching the types of people, following them round, observing them in their daily lives and remembering all the small details of action, gesture or expression which she could some day embody into a rôle.

The more one sees and studies people with sympathy, the more points one gets for the study of life which is embodied in the art one gives forth. But it is sympathy with one's fellow beings and kindly observation which help one here, never the critical attitude.

An artist can only afford to be coldly critical toward his own work and not toward the work of others.

Recently a young woman who started her vocal career as a contralto has sung the most difficult of Wagnerian soprano parts. Her high notes, it is true, were not the high notes of a natural soprano voice, but the care and perfection with which each high note was attacked were worthy of closest attention and admiration and defied criticism.

Hearing the smaller singers, the beginners who are still struggling with their art, should awaken in the heart of the intelligent listener not contemptuous criticism, but should be one means of realizing one's own vocal defects and the possible ways of overcoming them.

There are bad singing teachers, of course, but often the pupils are worse and will not listen to advice. The large and shrieking voice usually belongs to this type of pupil, for it is easier to force the voice when the temperament is robust and the vocal cords equally strong than it is to learn gently and quietly the correct and natural position in voice placement, and it is easier to make a noise as best you can than to use intelligently the different resonance cavities for the blending of the perfect tone.

Another fault severely criticised in the youthful singer is a lack of correct pronunciation or diction. It is only after the voice is perfectly controlled that the lips and tongue can function freely for the pronunciation of syllables.

While the voice is in what might be called a state of ferment the singer is only anxious to produce tones, and diction slips by the wayside. The appreciative listener should be able to know whether a lack of diction on the singer's part means immaturity or simply slovenliness.

Still another fault in voice production is the tremolo. It is the overambitious singer, the singer who forces a small, light organ to do heavy work, who develops the tremolo.

The tremolo is a sure sign that the vocal chords have been stretched beyond their natural limits, and there is only one thing can cure this. That is absolute rest for some time and then beginning the study of the voice, first singing with the mouth closed and relying entirely on very gentle breath pressure for the production of the sound.

The pupil suffering from tremolo or even very strong vibrato must have courage to stop at once and to forego having a big voice. After all, the most beautiful voices in the world are not necessarily the biggest voices, and certainly the tremolo is about the worst fault a singer can have. But that, like almost any other vocal defect, can be cured by persistent effort of the right kind.

In singing in public as well as when practicing the

singer must stand so that the body will be perfectly and firmly poised. One should always stand in such a position as to be able to inhale comfortably and control a large breath, to allow the throat absolute freedom, with the head sufficiently raised to let the inflowing air penetrate all the resonance cavities.

The great thing to avoid is stiffness or discomfort of any kind in the pose. At the same time one must have a gracious air, and while feeling perfectly solidly poised on the feet, must make the impression of a certain lightness and freedom from all bodily restraint.

I have not meant in these short articles to give you anything but a very general idea of the salient points of the art of singing. After all, each one must do the real work herself.

The road is full of discouragements and hardships, but there is always something new and interesting to learn, and to achieve success, whether for the public or merely for the home circle, is worth all the trouble one can take. And so I wish you all success.

ENRICO CARUSO

How a Neapolitan Mechanic's Son Became the
World's Greatest Tenor

ENRICO CARUSO enjoys the reputation of being the greatest tenor since Italo Campanini. The latter was the legitimate successor of Brignoli, an artist whose wonderful singing made his uncouth stage presence a matter of little moment. Caruso's voice at its best recalls Brignoli to the veteran opera habitué. It possesses something of the dead tenor's sweetness and clarity in the upper register, but it lacks the delicacy and artistic finish of Campanini's supreme effort, although it is vastly more magnetic and thrill inspiring.

That Caruso is regarded as the foremost living tenor is made good by the fact that he is the highest priced male artist in the world. Whenever and wherever he sings multitudes flock to hear him, and no one goes away unsatisfied. He is constantly the recipient of ovations which demonstrate the power of his min-strelsy, and his lack of especial physical attractiveness is no bar to the witchery of his voice.

Caruso is a Neapolitan and is now thirty-five years of age. Unlike so many great Italian tenors, he is not of peasant parentage. His father was a skilled mechanic who had been put in charge of the warehouses of a large banking and importing concern. As a lad Enrico used to frequent the docks in the vicinity of these warehouses and became an expert swimmer at a very early age. In those halcyon days his burning ambition was to be a sailor, and he had a profound distaste for his father's plan to have him learn a trade.

At the age of ten he was still a care free and fun loving boy, without a thought beyond the docks and their life. It was then that his father ruled that since he would not become a mechanic he must be sent to school. He had already learned to read a little, but that was all. He was sent to a day school in the neighborhood, and he accepted the restraint with such bad grace that he was in almost constant disgrace. His long association with the water front had made him familiar with the art of physical defense, and he was in frequent trouble on that account.

The head master of the school was a musician, and he discovered one day that his unruly pupil could sing. He was an expert in the development of the boy soprano and he soon realized that in young Caruso he had a veritable treasure. He was shrewd enough to keep his discovery to himself for some time, for he determined to profit by the boy's extraordinary ability. The lad was rehearsed privately and was stimulated to further effort by the promise of sweetmeats and release from school duties. Finally the unscrupulous master made engagements for the young prodigy to sing at fashionable weddings and concerts, but he always pocketed the money which came from these public appearances.

At the end of the second year, when Caruso was twelve years of age, he decided that he had had enough of the school, and he made himself so disagreeable to the head master that he was sent home in disgrace. His irate father gave him a sound thrashing and declared that he must be apprenticed to a mechanical engineer. The boy took little interest in his new work, but showed some aptitude for mechanical drawing and caligraphy. In a few months he became so interested in sketching that he began to indulge in visions of becoming a great artist.

When he was fifteen his mother died, and, since he had kept at the mechanical work solely on her account, he now announced his intention of forsaking engineering and devoting himself to art and music. When his father heard of this open rebellion he fell into a great rage and declared that he would have no more of him, that he was a disgrace to the family and that he need not show his face at home.

So Caruso became a wanderer, with nothing in his absolute possession save a physique that was perfect and an optimism that was never failing. He picked up a scanty livelihood by singing at church festivals and private entertainments and in time became known widely as the most capable boy soprano in Naples. Money came more plentifully, and he was able to live generously. In a short time his voice was transformed into a marvelous alto, and he soon found himself in great demand and was surfeited with attention from the rich and powerful. It was about this time that King Edward, then Prince of Wales, heard him sing in a Neapolitan church and was so delighted that he invited the boy to go to England, an invitation which young Caruso did not accept. Now that he had "arrived" Naples was good enough for him.

One day something happened which plunged him into the deepest despair. Without a warning of any sort his beautiful alto voice disappeared, leaving in its place only the feeblest and most unmusical of croaks. He was so overcome at his loss that he shut himself up in his room and would see no one. It was the first great affliction he had ever known, and he admits that he meditated suicide. He had made many friends, and some of them would have been glad to comfort him, but his grief would admit of no partnership.

One evening when he was skulking along an obscure highway, at the very bottom of the well of his despair, a firm hand was laid on his shoulder and a cheery voice called out: "Whither so fast? Come home with me, poor little shaver!"

It was Messiani, the famous baritone, who had always felt an interest in the boy and who would not release him in spite of his vigorous efforts to escape. The big baritone took him to his lodging and when he had succeeded in cheering the unhappy lad into a momentary forgetfulness of his misery asked him to sing.

"But I can't," sobbed Caruso. "It has gone!"

Messiani went to the piano and struck a chord. The weeping boy piped up in a tone so thin and feeble that it was almost indistinguishable.

"Louder!" yelled the big singer, with another full chord. Caruso obeyed and kept on through the scale. Then Messiani jumped up from the piano stool, seized the astonished boy about the waist and raised him high off his feet, at the same time yelling at the top of his voice: "What a little jackass! What a little idiot!"

Almost bursting with rage, for the miserable boy thought his friend was making sport of him, Caruso searched the apartment for some weapon with which he might avenge himself. Seizing a heavy brass candlestick, he hurled it at Messiani with all his force, but it missed the baritone and landed in a mirror.

"Hold, madman!" interposed the startled singer. "Your voice is not gone. It is magnificent. You will be the tenor of the century."

Messiani sent him to Vergine, then the most celebrated trainer of the voice in Italy. The maestro was not so enthusiastic as Messiani, but he promised to do what he could. He offered to instruct Caruso four years, only demanding 25 per cent. of his pupil's receipts for his first five years in opera. Caruso signed such a contract willingly, although he realized afterward that he was the victim of a veritable Shylock.

When Vergine was through with the young tenor he dismissed him without lavish commendation, but with a reminder of the terms of his contract. Caruso obtained an engagement in Naples, but did not achieve marked success at once. On every payday Vergine was on hand to receive his percentage. His regularity finally attracted the attention of the manager, and he made inquiry of Caruso. The young tenor showed him his copy of the contract and was horrified to be told that he had bound himself to his Shylock for a lifetime; that the contract read that he was to give Vergine five years of actual singing. Caruso would have reached the age of fifty before the last payment came. The matter was finally adjusted by the courts, and the unscrupulous teacher lost 200,000 lire by the judgment.

In Italy every man must serve his time in the army, and Caruso was checked in his operatic career by the call to go into barracks. Not long, however, was he compelled to undergo the tedium of army life. In consideration of his art he was permitted to offer his brother as a substitute after two months, and he returned to the opera. He was engaged immediately for a season at Caserta, and from that time his rise has been steady and unimpeded. After singing in one Italian city after another he went to Egypt and thence to Paris, where he made a favorable impression. A season in Berlin followed, but the Wagner influence was dominant, and he did not succeed in restoring the supremacy of Italian opera. The next season was spent in South America, and in the new world Caruso made his first triumph. From Rio he went to London, and on his first appearance he captured his Covent Garden audience. When he made his first appearance in the United States he was already at the top of the operatic ladder, and, although many attempts to dislodge him have been made, he stands still on the topmost rung.

O F the thousands of people who visit the opera during the season few outside of the small proportion of the initiated realize how much the performance of the singer whom they see and hear on the stage is dependent on previous rehearsal, constant practice and watchfulness over the physical conditions that preserve that most precious of our assets, the voice.

Nor does this same great public in general know of what the singer often suffers in the way of nervousness or stage fright before appearing in front of the footlights, nor that his life, outwardly so fêted and brilliant, is in private more or less of a retired, ascetic one and that his social pleasures must be strictly limited.

These conditions, of course, vary greatly with the individual singer, but I will try to tell in the following articles, as exemplified in my own case, what a great responsibility a voice is when one considers that it is the great God-given treasure which brings us our fame and fortune.

I am perhaps more favored than many in the fact that my voice was always "there," and that, with proper cultivation, of course, I have not had to overstrain it in the attempt to reach vocal heights which have come to some only after severe and long-continued effort. But, on the other hand, the finer the natural voice the more sedulous the care required to preserve it in its pristine freshness to bloom. This is the singer's ever present problem—in my case, however, mostly a matter of common sense living.

As regards eating—a rather important item, by the

way—I have kept to the light "continental" breakfast, which I do not take too early; then a rather substantial luncheon toward two o'clock. My native macaroni, specially prepared by my chef, who is engaged particularly for his ability in this way, is often a feature in this midday meal. I incline toward the simpler and more nourishing food, though my tastes are broad in the matter, but lay particular stress on the excellence of the cooking, for one cannot afford to risk one's health on indifferently cooked food, no matter what its quality.

On the nights when I sing I take nothing after luncheon, except perhaps a sandwich and a glass of Chianti, until after the performance, when I have a supper of whatever I fancy within reasonable bounds. Being blessed with a good digestion, I have not been obliged to take the extraordinary precautions about what I eat that some singers do. Still, I am careful never to indulge to excess in the pleasures of the table, for the condition of our alimentary apparatus and that of the vocal chords are very closely related, and the unhealthy state of the one immediately reacts on the other.

My reason for abstaining from food for so long before singing may be inquired. It is simply that when the large space required by the diaphragm in expanding to take in breath is partly occupied by one's dinner the result is that one cannot take as deep a breath as one would like and consequently the tone suffers and the all-important ease of breathing is interfered with. In addition a certain amount of bodily energy is used in the process of digestion which would otherwise be entirely given to the production of the voice.

These facts, seemingly so simple, are very vital ones to a singer, particularly on an "opening night." A singer's life is such an active one, with rehearsals and performances, that not much opportunity is given for "exercise," and the time given to this must, of course, be governed by individual needs. I find a few simple physical exercises in the morning after rising, somewhat similar to those practiced in the army, or the use for a few minutes of a pair of light dumbbells, very beneficial. Otherwise I must content myself with an occasional automobile ride. One must not forget, however, that the exercise of singing, with its constant deep inhalation (and acting in itself is considerable exercise also), tends much to keep one from acquiring an oversupply of embonpoint.

A proper moderation in eating, however, as I have already said, will contribute as much to the maintenance of correct proportion in one's figure as any amount of voluntary exercise which one only goes through with on principle.

As so many of you in a number of States of this great country are feeling and expressing as well as voting opinions on the subject of whether one should or should not drink intoxicants, you may inquire what practice is most in consonance with a singer's well being, in my opinion. Here, again, of course, customs vary with the individual. In Italy we habitually drink the light wines of the country with our meals and surely are never the worse for it. I have retained my fondness for my native Chianti, which I have even made on my own Italian estate, but believe and carry out the belief that moderation is the only possible course. I am inclined to condemn the use of spirits, whisky in particular, which is so prevalent in the Anglo-Saxon countries, for it is sure to inflame the delicate little ribbons of tissue which produce the singing tone and then— *addio* to a clear and ringing high C!

Though I indulge occasionally in a cigarette, I advise all singers, particularly young singers, against this practice, which can certainly not fail to have a bad effect on the delicate lining of the throat, the vocal chords and the lungs.

You will see by all the foregoing that even the gift of a good breath is not to be abused or treated lightly, and that the "goose with the golden egg" must be most carefully nurtured.

Outside of this, however, one of the great temptations that beset any singer of considerable fame is the many social demands that crowd upon him, usually unsought and largely undesired. Many of the invitations to receptions, teas and dinners are from comparative strangers and cannot be considered, but of those from one's friends which it would be a pleasure to attend very few indeed can be accepted, for the singer's first care, even if a selfish one, must be for his health and consequently his voice, and the attraction of social intercourse must, alas, be largely foregone.

The continual effort of loud talking in a throng would be extremely bad for the sensitive musical instrument that the vocalist carries in his throat, and the various beverages offered at one of your afternoon teas it would be too difficult to refuse. So I confine myself to an occasional quiet dinner with a few friends on an off night at the opera or any evening at the play, where I can at least be silent during the progress of the acts.

In common with most of the foreign singers who come to America, I have suffered somewhat from the effects of your barbarous climate, with its sudden changes of temperature, but perhaps have become more accustomed to it in the years of my operatic work here. What has affected me most, however, is the overheating of the houses and hotels with that dry steam heat which is so trying to the throat. Even when I took a house for the season I had difficulty in keeping the air moist. Now, however, in the very modern and excellent hotel where I am quartered they have a new system of ventilation by which the air is automatically rendered pure and the heat controlled—a great blessing to the over-sensitive vocalist.

After reading the above the casual person will perhaps believe that a singer's life is really not a bit of a sinecure, even when he has attained the measure of this world's approval and applause afforded by the "great horse-shoe."

THE question, "How is it done?" as applied to the art of singing brings up so many different points that it is difficult to know where to begin or how to give the layman in any kind of limited space a concise idea of the principles controlling the production of the voice and their application to vocal art.

Every singer or singing master is popularly supposed to have a method by following out which he has come to fame. Yet if asked to describe this method many an artist would be at a loss to do so, or else deny that he had any specific method at all, such a subtle and peculiarly individual matter it is that constitutes the technical part of singing. Most singers—in fact, all of them—do many things in singing habitually, yet so inconspicuously that they could not describe how or why they did them. Yet this little set of "artistic" habits all arise from most logical causes and have become habits from their fitness to the personality of their owner and their special value in enabling that singer to do his best work by their aid. For instance, a singer will know from trials and experience just the proper position of the tongue and larynx to produce most effectively a certain note on the scale, yet he will have come by this knowledge not by theory and reasoning, but simply oft repeated attempts, and the knowledge he has come by will be valuable to him only, for somebody else would produce the same note equally well, but in quite a different way.

So one may see that there are actually as many methods as there are singers, and any particular method, even if accurately set forth, might be useless to the person who tried it. This is what I really would reply to anyone putting this question to me—that my own particular way of singing, if I have any, is, after all, peculiarly suited to me only, as I have above described.

However, there are many interesting and valuable things to be said about the voice in a general way.

Speaking first of the classification of voices, many young singers are put much in doubt and dilemma because they are unable to determine what sort of voice they really possess, whether soprano, mezzo or contralto. Of course, it is easy enough to distinguish between the extremes of these, between a "real" tenor and a low bass, but the difference between a high baritone and tenor is rather more difficult to discern, and a young man studying has often been at great disadvantage by imagining, for instance, that he had a tenor voice and trying constantly to sing music too high for him, since he in reality had only a high baritone.

In the course of development a voice very often increases its range and changes its quality sufficiently to pass from a baritone to a tenor, and it is sometimes a problem to place it during the transition process. Perhaps the surest way to determine the real character of a voice is to see on what notes words can be most easily pronounced. For the average tenor the notes up to A above middle C, for the baritone, D above middle C, and for the bass up to middle C itself, can be pronounced on the best.

One should never try to change the tessitura, or natural character of the voice. A voice will become higher just when it should by the development due to rational work and never by forcing it. Nothing is easier than to force a voice upward or downward, but to cause it to "recede," as it were, in either direction, is another matter. A baritone who tries to increase his upper range by main strength will surely in time lose his best lower notes, and a light tenor who attempts to force out notes lower than his range will never be able to sing legitimate tenor roles, and after two or three years may not be able to sing at all.

It may be well to speak now of a very important point in singing—what is called the "attack" of the tone. In general this may be described as the relative position of the throat and tongue and the quality of voice as the tone is begun. The most serious fault of many singers is that they attack the tone either from the chest or the throat. Even with robust health the finest voice cannot resist this. This is the reason one sees so many artists who have made a brilliant debut disappear from sight very soon or wind up later on a mediocre career. Singers who use their voices properly should be at the height of their talents at forty-five and keep their voices in full strength and virility up to at least fifty. At this latter age, or close after it, it would seem well to have earned the right to close one's career.

A great artist ought to have the dignity to say farewell to his public when still in full possession of his powers and never let the world apprise him of his falling off.

To have the attack true and pure one must consciously try to open the throat not only in front, but from behind, for the throat is the door through which the voice must pass, and if it is not sufficiently open it is useless to attempt to get out a full, round one; also the throat is the outlet and inlet for the breath, and if it is closed the voice will seek other channels or return quenched within.

It must not be imagined that to open the mouth wide

will do the same for the throat.   If one is well versed
in the art, one can open the throat perfectly without
a perceptible opening of the mouth, merely by the
power of respiration.

It is necessary to open the sides of the mouth, at the
same time dropping the chin well, to obtain good throat
opening. In taking higher notes, of course, one must open
the mouth a little wider, but for the most part the
position of the mouth is that assumed when smiling.
It is a good idea to practice opening the throat before
a mirror and try to see the palate, as when you show
your throat to a doctor.

In pronouncing the sound "ah" one must always
attack it in the back part of the throat, taking care,
however, before uttering the syllable, to have the
throat well open; otherwise what is called "stroke of
the glottis" occurs and the tone formed is hard and
disagreeable.   If you ever hear this stroke of glottis on
the attack, you may know that the singer did not attack
far enough back in the throat.

The tone once launched, one must think how it may
be properly sustained, and this is where the art of
breathing is most concerned.   The lungs, in the first
place, should be thoroughly filled.   A tone begun with
only half filled lungs loses half its authority and is very
apt to be false in pitch.   To take a full breath properly,
the chest must be raised at the same moment the abdomen sinks in.   Then with the gradual expulsion of
the breath a contrary movement takes place.   The
diaphragm and elastic tissue surrounding and containing
the stomach and vital organs and the muscles surrounding, by practice acquire great strength and assist con-
siderably in this process of respiration and are vital
factors in the matter of controlling the supply which

supports the tone.   The diaphragm is really like a pair
of bellows and serves exactly the same purpose.   It
is this ability to take in an adequate supply of breath
and to retain it until required that makes or, by contrary, mars all singing.   A singer with a perfect sense
of pitch and all the good intentions possible will often
sing off the key and bring forth a tone with no vitality
to it, distressing to hear, simply for lack of breath control.

This art of respiration once acquired, the student has
gone a considerable step on the road to Parnassus.

To practice deep breathing effectively it is an excellent plan to breathe through the nose, which aids in
keeping the confined breath from escaping too soon.
The nose also warms and filters the air, making it much
more agreeable to the lungs than if taken directly
through the mouth.   In the practice of slow breathing
make sure that the lungs are as nearly emptied as possible on the expulsion of the breath before beginning a
new inspiration, as this gives extra impetus to the fresh
supply of air and strengthens all the breathing muscles.

If this is not done, moreover, the effect is like two
people trying to get in and out of the same narrow door
at the same time.

The voice is naturally divided into three registers—
the chest, medium and head.   In a man's voice of lower
quality this last is known as "falsetto," but in the case
of a tenor he may use a tone which in sound is almost
falsetto, but is really a mezza voce, or half voice.   This
latter legitimately belongs to a man's compass; a falsetto
does not.   The most important register is the medium,
particularly of tenors, for this includes the greater part
of the tenor's voice and can be utilized even to the top
of his range if rightly produced.

In the matter of taking high notes one should remember that their purity and ease of production depend very much on the way the preceding notes leading up to them are sung. Beginning in the lower register and attacking the ascending notes well back, a balance must be maintained all the way up, so that the highest note receives the benefit and support of the original position of the throat, and there is no danger, consequently, of the throat closing and pinching the quality of the top notes.

Singers, especially tenors, are very apt to throw the head forward in producing the high notes, and consequently get that throaty, strained voice which is so disagreeable. To avoid this one should try to keep the supply of breath down as far toward the abdomen as possible, thus maintaining the upper passages to the head quite free for the emission of the voice. Remember also to sing within yourself, as it were—to feel the tones all through your being; otherwise your singing will possess no sentiment, emotion or authority. It is the failure to accomplish this which has produced so many soulless artists—singers endowed with magnificent voices, capable of surmounting every technical difficulty, but devoid of that charm of intonation which is so vital to success on the operatic stage.

Faults to be Corrected

I HAVE previously mentioned mezza voce and will now say a word on this subject, for the artistic use of the "half voice" is a very valuable adjunct in all singing. It may be defined simply as the natural voice produced softly, but with an extra strength of breath. It is this breathy quality, however—which one must be careful never to exaggerate or the tone will not carry—that gives that velvety effect to the tone that is so delightful.

Mezza voce is just a concentration of the full voice, and it requires, after all, as much breath support. A soft note which is taken with the "head voice" without being supported by a breath taken from the diaphragm is a helpless sort of thing. It does not carry and is inaudible at any distance, whereas the soft note which does possess the deep breath support is penetrating, concentrated and most expressive.

Another important point is that, with a "piano" note properly taken in the register which is proper to it, there is no danger of having to change the position of the throat and consequently the real character of the note when making a crescendo and again diminishing it. It will be the same note continuing to sound.

On the other hand, with a soft note taken in a register foreign to it, as soon as its strength is augmented the register must suddenly be changed and the result is like a Tyrolean yodel.

So remember in a mezza voce to see that the register is right and to use a double breath strength. I speak of the matter of register here for the benefit of those who must keep this constantly in mind.   I myself have been blessed with what is called a naturally placed voice, and never had trouble with the mezza voce.   The majority of Italian singers come to it easily.

There are a number of wrong sorts of voices which should be mentioned to be shunned—the "white" voice, the "throaty" voice, the "nasal" voice, and the "bleat."   The nasal quality is the most difficult to correct.   Many teachers, especially the French, make a point of placing the voice in the nasal cavity on the pretext of strengthening it, and this nasal quality, partly on account of the sound of many of the French words, is only too prevalent.   The voice, however, can only be strengthened by legitimate means; otherwise it can easily be ruined.   One can breathe through the nose, but never attack or sing through it.

The "white voice" (voce bianca) is a head voice without deep support and consequently without color; hence its appellation.   One can learn to avoid it by practicing with the mouth closed and by taking care to breathe through the nose, which forces the respiration to descend to the abdomen.

The "throaty" voice comes from singing with the throat insufficiently opened, so that the breath does not pass easily through the nose and head cavities and, again, from not attacking the tone deeply enough.

To cure oneself of this throaty quality attack your notes from the abdomen, the mouth well open, standing in front of a mirror.   The force of the respiration will keep the tongue depressed and the throat will remain free.

As for the fault of nasality, it is, as I have said, the most difficult to get rid of.   Sometimes one never does lose it.   The only remedy is what I have previously indicated—to attack from the abdomen, with the throat open, and carry the voice over the soft palate, for if the voice is placed in the nose it indicates that one is singing too far forward, which is against the rules of song.   If the student has a tendency to sing in this way it is well to practice in vowel sounds only (ah-eh-ee-la-lay-lee, etc.) in order to be cured of this serious fault.

After all, however, those who have practiced the art of right breathing need have none of the defects mentioned above.

The "bleat" or goat voice, a particular fault of French singers, proceeds from the habit of forcing the voice, which, when it is of small volume, cannot stand the consequent fatigue of the larynx.   Many singers with voices suitable only for light opera are constantly trying to branch out into big dramatic arias.   Such performances are assuredly distressing to hear and are certainly disastrous for the voices concerned.   It is no wonder that these people are often ill, for one cannot make such efforts without injuring the health.   I realize that they often do it to please their directors and to be obliging in an emergency, but when they are down and out others will easily replace them and they are heard from no more.

To keep the voice fresh for the longest possible time one should not only never overstep his vocal "means," but should limit his output as he does the expenses of his purse.

There is only one way to cure a bleaty voice, and that is to cultivate an absolute rest; then, on taking up singing again, to use the "closed mouth" method until the time the strength of respiration shall be such that one can open his mouth and let the restored voice take its course.

A few words on practicing with closed mouth may here be appropriate. This method of study is really all that is necessary to place certain voices, but is bad for others. It all depends on the formation of the mouth and throat. For example, a singer troubled with the fault of closing the throat too much should never work with the mouth closed. When one can do it safely, however, it is a most excellent resource for preparatory exercises in respiration. Since, as I have already explained, breathing through the nose with closed mouth throws back the respiration to the abdomen, it is best to do the exercise seated in a comfortable, natural position.

Vocal work with closed mouth is also a powerful auxiliary to vocal agility. Many great artists perform their daily vocal exercises with the mouth shut, and I can personally testify to the excellency of this practice. It most certainly strengthens the breathing powers and at the same time rests the voice. But one should know how to do it properly. I know of many badly fatigued voices that have been restored to their normal condition in this way.

Singers, of all musicians, have the reputation of displaying the least regard for time. In operatic work, however, with an orchestra to follow or be followed, it is especially essential to observe a sane respect for the proper tempo. Otherwise one is liable to get into immediate trouble with the conductor. Of course I do not mean that one should sing in a mechanical way and give nothing of one's own personality. This would naturally rob the music of all charm. There are many singers who cannot or will not count the time properly. There are those who sing without method, who do not fit their breathing, which is really the regulator of vocal performance, to the right periods, and who consequently are never in time. They make all kinds of rallentandos where they are not necessary, to gain time to recover the breath that they have not taken when they should. It is not enough to give the notes their full value. The rests, above all, should be carefully observed in order to have sufficient opportunity to get a good breath and prepare for the next phrase. It is this exactitude that gives certainty to one's rendition and authority in singing—something many artists do not possess. A singer may make all the efforts he desires and still keep the time, and he *must* keep it.

Those who roar most loudly rarely sing in time. They give every thought to the volume of tone they are producing and do not bother themselves about anything else. The right accents in music depend very much on the exact time. Tone artists, while still making all their desired "effects" in apparent freedom of style and delivery, nevertheless do not ever lose sight of the time. Those who do are usually apt to be amateurs and are not to be imitated.

Good Diction a Requisite

GOOD diction, or the art of pronouncing the words of a song or opera properly and intelligently, is a matter sadly neglected by many singers, and indeed is not considered important by a large proportion of the audiences in this country, who do not understand foreign language, at any rate. And in an opera sung in a language unknown to most of the audience it is apparently unimportant whether the words are understood or not as long as there is a general knowledge of the plot, and the main consideration is, of course, the music.

Yet for those who are conversant with the language in which the opera is written, how common an experience it is (in concert, also) to be able, in spite of their linguistic knowledge, to understand little of what is being sung, and what a drawback this really is! How many singers there are who seem to turn all their attention to the production of beautiful sounds and neglect in most cases the words that often are equally beautiful, or should be!

One hears a great deal just now about the advisability of giving operas in the native language, as it is done in France and Germany, and the idea would seem to have its advantages, as has already been demonstrated in some excellent performances of German, French and Italian operas in English. But of what avail would such a project be if, after all, one could not understand the words of his own language as they were sung?

The language might as well be Sanskrit or Chinese.

In France the matter of diction is probably given the greatest attention, and singers at the Opera Comique, for instance, are noted for their pure and distinct enunciation of every syllable.   Indeed, it is as much of a sine qua non there as good singing, if not more so, and the numerous subtleties in the French language are difficult enough to justify this special stress laid upon correct pronunciation.

It requires a very particular ability in a foreigner to attain the atmosphere of perfect French to any very high degree.   Italian is generally considered an easier language to pronounce in song, as indeed it is, all the vowel sounds being full and sonorous and lacking that "covered" or mixed quality so often occurring in the French.   Nevertheless, Italian has its difficulties, particularly in the way of distinctly enunciating the double consonants and proper division of the liaisons, or combining of final vowels with initial vowels, and the correct amount of softness to be given to the letter C.

All this, of course, is from the standpoint of those to whom these languages are foreign.

Certainly no singer can be called a great artist unless his diction is good, for a beautiful voice alone will not make up for other deficiencies.   A singer endowed with a small voice or even one of not very pleasing quality can give more pleasure than a singer possessing a big, impressive voice, but no diction.

Some people claim that a pronunciation too distinct or too much insisted upon spoils the real voice quality, but this should not be the case if the words are correctly and naturally brought out.   Doubtless, this impression has come from the fact that, particularly in France, many singers possessed of small voices must exaggerate their diction to obtain their effects.   But if they did not have this perfect diction they often would have little else to recommend them. I would aver that a fine enunciation, far from interfering with it, aids the voice production, makes it softer and more concentrated, but diction should act rather as a frame for the voice and never replace it.

Each of the three languages, French, German and Italian, has its peculiar characteristics, which are of aid to the student in the general study of pronunciation, and it is well to have a knowledge of them all outside of the fact that an artist nowadays needs to have this knowledge in order not only to rank with the greatest, but to cope with the demands of an operatic career.

The Italian language in its very essence is rich in vowels and vowel combinations, from which comes principally the color in tones, and it has consequently been called the "language of song." Italians thus have naturally what it is so much trouble for singers of other nations to acquire—the numerous variations of vowel sounds.

French has the nasal sounds as its dominating characteristic and is very valuable in the cultivation of "nasal resonance."

As I said before, it is so easy to exaggerate and the voice is so apt to get too much "in the nose" that one has to be extremely careful in the use of the French "n" and "ng."

German is so full of consonants that one needs to have exceptional control of the tongue and lips to give their proper value.

English possesses the features of all the other languages—of course, in less marked degree— resembling most, perhaps, the German. The "th" is the most difficult sound to make effective in singing.

I have already spoken of the various phases of nervousness which an artist feels before the performance, but I wish to say here a word in regard to the practical significance of such nervousness. Artists who do not experience it are those who lack real genius. There are really two kinds of fear—that arising from a realization of the importance of what is to be done, the other from a lack of confidence in one's power. If a singer has no conscience in his performance he is never nervous, but full of assurance.

It is seldom that true artists are much troubled with nervousness after going upon the stage. Generally, as I have before mentioned, they are apt to be ill during the day of the performance, but before the public they forget everything and are dominated only by the real love of their art and sustained by the knowledge of possessing a proper " method."

It is certain with a good breath support even nervousness need not prevent one from singing well, although one may be actually suffering from trepidation. Yet we know that sometimes the greatest of artists are prevented thus from doing their best work. The principle, however, remains unshaken that singing in a correct way is the greatest possible " bracer."

It is best to remain absolutely quiet and see no one on the day of the performance, so as not to be enervated by the effort of talking much, to say nothing of tiring the vocal chords. One prima donna of my acquaintance occupies herself in trimming hats on the day when she sings, believing that this provides a distraction and rests her nerves. It is just as well not to " pass through" the rôle that is to be sung on the day of the appearing, but in the morning a few technical exercises to keep the voice in tune, as it were, are to be recommended. The great Italian singers of other days followed this rule, and it still holds good.

If the singer gives much of himself as well as of his voice to the public he should still hold his breathing supply in, so to speak, as he would guard the capital from which comes his income. Failure should thus be impossible if there is always a reserve to draw on. So the more one sings with good breath support the more beautiful the voice becomes. On the other hand, those who sing haphazard sometimes begin the evening well, but deteriorate more and more as the performance advances and at the end are uttering mere raucous sounds. They are like a man unable to swim who is in a deep river—their voices control them in place of they controlling their voices. They struggie vainly against obstacles, but are carried away by the flood and are finally engulfed in the waters.

Many too ambitious students are their own worst enemies in the culture of their voices. Because they have a large vocal power they want to shout all the time in spite of the repeated admonitions of their masters, who beg them to sing piano. But they hear nothing except the noise they make themselves. Such headstrong ones will never make a career, even with the finest voices in the world. Their teachers should give up trying to make them listen to reason and devote their attention to those who merit it and want to study seriously. Singing as an art is usually not considered with enough earnestness. One should go to a singing master as one goes to a specialist for a consultation and follow with the greatest care his directions. If one does not have the same respect and confidence one places in a physician it must be because the singing master does not really merit it, and it would be much better to make a change at once.

In general it is better not to stick entirely to one teacher, for it is easy to get into a rut in this way, and someone else may have a quite different and more enlightening way of setting forth his ideas.

In taking up operatic work it is understood, of course, that the singer must have mastered most of the technical difficulties, so as not to be troubled with them when they are encountered in some aria.

It is a most excellent thing to secure an engagement in one of the small theatres abroad, where one may get a large experience before trying to effect an entrance into the bigger organizations of the great capitals.

But be sure that the voice is well placed before trying any of this sort of work, and never attempt to sing a rôle above your powers in the earlier stage of your career, which otherwise may be compromised permanently.

One more bit of advice in closing. The best sort of lesson possible is to go often to the opera and note well the methods of the great artists. This personal example is worth more and is more illuminating than many precepts.

This is not so much that any form of imitation may be attempted as to teach the would-be artist how to present at his best all those telling qualities with which he may be endowed. It is the best of schools.

THE most visible phase of the opera singer's life when he or she is in view of the public on the stage is naturally the one most intimately connected in the minds of the majority of people with the singer's personality, and yet there are many happenings, amusing or tragic, from the artist's point of view, which, though often seen, are as often not realized in their true significance by the audience in front of the orchestra. One might naturally think that a singer who has been appearing for years on the operatic stage in many lands would have overcome or outgrown that bane of all public performers, stage fright. Yet such is far from the case, for it seems as though the greater the artistic temperament the more truly the artist feels and the more of himself he puts into the music he sings the greater his nervousness beforehand. The latter is of course augmented if the performance is a first night and the opera has as yet been untried before a larger public.

This advance state of miserable physical tension is the portion of all great singers alike, though in somewhat varying degrees, and it is interesting to note the forms it assumes with different people. In many it is shown by excessive irritability and the disposal to pick quarrels with anyone who comes in contact with them. This is an unhappy time for the luckless "dressers," wig man and stage hands, or even fellow artists who encounter such singers before their first appearance in the evening. Trouble is the portion of all such.

In other artists the state of mind is indicated by a

67

stern set countenance and a ghastly pallor, while still
others become slightly hysterical, laugh uproariously at
nothing or burst into weeping.   I have seen a big six-
foot bass singer, very popular at the opera two or three
seasons ago, walking to and fro with the tears running
down his cheeks for a long time before his entrance, and
one of our greatest coloratura prima donnas has come
to me before the opera, sung a quavering note in a voice
full of emotion and said, with touching accents: "See,
that is the best I can do.   How can I go on so?"

I myself have been affected often by such fright,
though not always in the extreme degree above described.   This nervousness, however, frequently shows
itself in one's performance in the guise of indifferent
acting, singing off the key, etc.   Artists are generally
blamed for such shortcomings, apparent in the early
part of the production, when, as a matter of fact, they
themselves are hardly conscious of them and overcome
them in the course of the evening.   Yet the public,
even critics, usually forget this fact and condemn an
entire performance for faults which are due at the
beginning to sheer nervousness.

The oft-uttered complaint that operatic singers are
the most difficult to get on with of any folk, while
justified, perhaps, can certainly be explained by the
foregoing observations.

We of the opera are often inclined to be superstitious
in a way that might annul matter of fact Americans.
One woman, a distinguished and most intelligent artist,
crosses herself repeatedly before taking her "cue," and a
prima donna who is a favorite on two continents and
who is always escorted to the theatre by her mother,
invariably goes through the very solemn ceremony of
kissing her mother good-by and receiving her blessing

before going on to sing. The young woman feels that she could not possibly sing a note if the mother's eye were not on her every moment from the wings.

Another famous singer wears a small bracelet that was given to her when an infant by Gounod. She has grown somewhat stout of late years, and the hoop of gold has been reenforced so often that there is hardly any of the great composer's original gift left. Still, she feels that it is a charm which has made her success, and whether she sings the part of a lowly peasant or of a princess the bracelet is always visible.

And these little customs are not confined to the woman singers either, for the men are equally fond of observing some little tradition to cheer them in their performance. These little traits, trivial perhaps in themselves, are of vital importance in that they create a sense of security in the soul of the artist, who goes on his way, if not rejoicing, at least convinced that the fates are not against him.

One of the penalties paid by the singers who are much in the public eye is the constant demand made on them to listen to voices of vocal aspirants—not always very young ones, strange to say. It is sad to contemplate the number of people who think they can sing and are destined by talent and temperament for operatic careers, who have been led by misguided or foolish friends and too often by overambitious and mercenary singing masters into spending time and money on their voices in the fond hope of some day astonishing the world. Alas, they do not realize that the great singers who are heard in the New York opera houses have been picked from the world's supply after a process of most drastic selection, and that it is only the most rarely exceptional voice and talent which after long years of study and preparation become worthy to join the elect.

I am asked to hear many who have voices with promise of beauty, but who have obviously not the intelligence necessary to take up a career, for it does require considerable intelligence to succeed in opera, in spite of opinions to the contrary expressed by many. Others, who have keen and alert minds and voices of fine quality, yet lack that certain esprit and broadness of musical outlook required in a great artist. This lack is often so apparent in the person's manner or bearing that I am tempted to tell him it is no use before he utters a note. Yet it would not do to refuse a hearing to all these misfits, for there is always the chance of encountering the unknown genius, however rare a bird he may be.

And how often have the world's great voices been discovered by chance, but fortunately by some one empowered to bring out the latent gift!

One finds in America many beautiful voices, and when one thinks of the numerous singers successfully engaged in operatic careers both here and abroad, it cannot with justice be said as it used to be several years ago that America does not produce opera singers. Naturally a majority of those to whom I give a hearing here in New York are Americans, and of these are a number of really remarkable voices and a fairly good conception of what is demanded of an opera singer.

Sometimes, however, it would be amusing if it were not tragic to see how much off the track people are who have been led to think they have futures. One young man who came recently to sing for me carried a portentous roll of music and spoke in the deepest of bass voices. When asked what his main difficulty was he replied that he "didn't seem to be able to get on the key." And this was apparent when he started in and wandered up and down the tonal till he managed to strike the tonic. Then he asked me whether I would rather hear "Qui sdegno," from Mozart's "Magic Flute," or "Love Me and the World is Mine." Upon the latter being chosen he asked the accompanist to transpose it, and upon this gentleman's suggesting a third lower, he said: "No, put it down an octave." And that's where he sang it, too. I gently but firmly advised the young man to seek other paths than musical ones. However, such extreme examples as that are happily rare.

I would say to all young people who are ambitious to enter on a career of opera: Remember, it is a thoroughly hard-worked profession, after all; that even with a voice of requisite size and proper cultivation there is still a repertory of rôles to acquire, long months and years of study for this and requiring a considerable feat of memory to retain them even after they are learned. Then there is the art of acting to be studied, which is, of course, an entire occupation in itself and decidedly necessary in opera, including fencing—how to fall properly, the various gaits and gestures wherewith to portray different emotions, etc. Then, as opera is sung nowadays, the knowledge of the diction of at least three languages—French, German and Italian—if not essential, is at least most helpful.

HOW TO SING

LUISA TETRAZZINI

HOW TO SING

BY

LUISA TETRAZZINI

CONTENTS

v

CONTENTS

HOW TO SING

HOW TO SING

CHAPTER I

DON'T WAIT TO BE "FOUND"

EVERY day of my life I receive letters from
men and women, mostly women, whom I do
not know personally, asking me to advise them
how best to use their vocal talents. Some of my
correspondents also request me to give them an
audition so that they can demonstrate their claim
to be embryonic stars.

It is manifestly impossible for me to spend all
my time listening to persons unknown to me, in
the hope of finding new Carusos, new Pattis and,
shall I say it?—new Tetrazzinis. If I were to do
so I should have little time for my own practice.
Nevertheless, whenever I am able, I do give an
audition to a young aspirant to musical fame, as
I consider it my duty to help, to the best of my
ability, those who are to come after me.

To those correspondents whom I have been unable to see personally let me say that star singers
are not necessarily discovered by stars. It is

quite true that from time to time it has been my fortunate experience to discover a tenor or a baritone or a soprano. But they had already been more or less discovered before I found them.

True at Covent Garden I found John McCormack singing a very minor rôle and was instrumental in having him elevated to the position of principal tenor. And other *prime donne* have acted similarly.

Nevertheless these artists would doubtless have come to the front in their own time without being "discovered" by a *prima donna*. Most big artists of to-day were not found by any one: they found themselves. I, for instance, was nobody's find. When the *prima donna* failed to appear at the opening night of an opera in my native Florence I volunteered to take the part, and in so doing discovered myself.

My readers will therefore understand that to be discovered by a great singer is not essential to becoming a great artist, and that because I am unable to give auditions to all who ask me I am not hindering them from becoming successful.

But for the benefit of those numerous correspondents who have expressed to me a desire that I should help all interested in training their voices, especially in their attempts to climb the difficult ladder of successful singing in public, I have consented to publish the following hints, and I hope sincerely they will be useful to all who read them.

I do not claim that I have given an exhaustive treatise—no one ever has done so—on the art of singing, but I am sure that any one possessing a voice who cares to put into practice the suggestions I am now making, will be benefited thereby.

From this handbook I have purposely excluded the story of my professional life. That is already published under the title of "My Life of Song" (Cassell and Co., London; Dorrance, Philadelphia, U. S. A.).

It will be observed that I use the word "he" all the way through when meaning "he or she." This is merely because I understand there is no English word which expresses the both. It would have been more modern to have used "she" in every case, but perhaps less modest. My lady readers will, however, understand that I am writing at least as much, if not more, for their benefit than for our lords and masters.

Chapter II

YOUR AIM

SINGERS may be divided into two classes. No, I do not mean, as some might suppose, those who can sing and those who cannot, though that is a possible classification. I mean in this case those who sing for mere pleasure and those who intend to make a career in this way. It is for both that these pages are intended.

As we have often been told, whatever is worth doing at all is worth doing well, and there is no reason why the singers who practise our beautiful art only for the enjoyment of themselves and their friends should not make the most of the powers which the good God has given them. I think, indeed, that it is their plain duty to do so, if only in the interests of their hearers. And I am glad to think that nowadays many see the matter in this light.

However it may be in the case of professional singers—upon which point I shall have something to say presently—there is, I suppose, no doubt that the standard of amateur singing has enormously improved during recent years.

The days when it was thought that anyone, however poorly equipped, had the right to stand up and perform in public, have passed away, and in those circles, at all events, where there is any kind of pretension to general intelligence and culture it is expected that all who come forward in this way shall show themselves to be possessed of at least some knowledge of the rudiments of the art.

As to the general necessity for study on the part of those who aspire to sing, few words, I suppose, are necessary. If every one can sing after a fashion, there is, I venture to say, no branch of the art of music which demands a more arduous apprenticeship and more prolonged study, if all of its higher possibilities are to be realised.

Precisely, however, because singing is in itself such a purely natural proceeding, this elementary fact is too often overlooked. "Singing," it has been well said, "derives its power from nature, but owes its perfection to art," and this is a fact which, I am afraid, is too often forgotten.

People, who would not dream of attempting to play the violin or give a piano solo in public without thorough preparation, will have no hesitation in standing up and attempting to sing, although they may be just as little qualified in the one case as in the other. They do not realise that the voice is, in reality, one of the most delicate and difficult of all instruments and demands in consequence no less study and practice than any other before it can be really artistically employed.

There is, moreover, another aspect of the singer's art which should never be forgotten. I allude to the fact that the singer is necessarily a reproductive artist—one whose business it is from the nature of the case to reproduce and interpret the music of others.

This imposes a duty and an obligation which should never be lost sight of. A singer has not only his own reputation to consider, but also that of the composer whose music he interprets, and for this reason alone, therefore, he can never take his art too seriously.

As to those contemplating a professional career, no words of mine will be necessary, I hope, to impress upon them the necessity of the sternest self-discipline and the most unremitting application if they are ever to succeed in accomplishing anything worth doing.

Chapter III

WHY SINGERS ARE SCARCE

THE career of a singer is one offering a certain number of prizes but many, many blanks, and only those possessed of the most unmistakable natural gifts and ready to work tremendously hard should ever be encouraged to embark upon it. Hard work, beyond everything, is essential if success is to be achieved, and it is here, I am afraid, that so many of our modern students fail.

Imbued with the eager impatient spirit of these headlong days, they want to do things too quickly, and are unwilling to submit to the toil and drudgery which are none the less as necessary as ever if really solid results are to be achieved. It has even been suggested that to this circumstance may be traced that scarcity of great singers nowadays of which we hear so often.

True, more vocalists than ever before, probably, are inviting attention at the present time, but how few of them can be reckoned in the first class? Doubtless it is easy to exaggerate in this matter. Seen through the mists of time the figures of the past always tend to assume heroic proportions.

Making due allowance, however, in this respect, are we really the victims of hallucination in thinking that great singers are fewer nowadays than formerly? It would be pleasant to think so, but I am afraid that the facts point the other way.

What, then, is the explanation? Different authorities would doubtless suggest different answers, but most, I fancy, would agree that lack of adequate study has had not a little to do with the matter.

Porpora, we all know, kept Caffarelli for five years to one page of exercises, and at the end of that time told him that he was the greatest singer in Europe. It would be amusing to learn the experience of a modern teacher who proposed to one of his pupils the adoption of the same course. The great Patti, who told me I was her successor, also said to me that we artists will still be learning when we are too old to sing.

The average vocal student of to-day considers himself a finished artist at a time when he would be reckoned just qualified to begin serious study by the teachers of an earlier period.

While no amount of training will make fine voices out of poor material, the history of singing furnishes numerous instances—that of Pasta is one of the best known—in which limited natural powers have been developed to an astonishing degree by study and training. Nowadays I am afraid it is the converse of this which is more frequently illustrated, and one hears only too often of fine natural voices which have been steadily ruined by the manner in which they are used.

Modern music has also, no doubt, had its influence—not so much because it is harmful to the voice in itself, but simply because it is possible to sing it (after a fashion) without such prolonged study and exercise as that of the older school absolutely necessitated.

Rossini, Donizetti, Bellini, and the rest of the old masters have indeed been avenged in a wholly unanticipated manner. Precisely as the music of their school has fallen in favour has the power been lost of singing that of the so-called higher kind which has taken its place.

CHAPTER IV

PERIOD OF TRAINING

FOR this melancholy state of affairs the only remedy is a return to sounder views. The fact must be recognised that there are no short cuts to perfection in singing any more than in any other art, and that those who wish to sing like the great ones of the past must be prepared to work and study as they did, in order to attain this end.

What period of training should be considered sufficient to equip a vocal student? In former days eight, nine, or even ten years were not considered too much for this purpose. I need hardly say how very different are the views prevailing nowadays, when students consider themselves qualified to appear in public at the end of a year or two of hasty and necessarily superficial training. Needless to say, no satisfactory results can possibly be achieved in this length of time. I consider a minimum of four years necessary to become a professional singer.

Lilli Lehmann has put the matter happily. At least six years, she says, should be considered the minimum period allowable—to which, she says further, there should then be added an entire lifetime for further study and improvement!

This is not to say that many great singers have not perfected their art and even attained the very highest positions in a much shorter time. In my own case my period of actual systematic training in the strict sense of the term was comparatively brief—six months. But then in another sense I was learning from my childhood. Moreover, I was exceptionally lucky in that my voice was pitched just right, and had not to be trained to do what is usually regarded as difficult.

Almost from my infancy it was my ambition to become an operatic singer, and circumstances enabled me to benefit to the utmost extent by the constant hearing of opera, and also the constant criticism of singers by competent judges, so that I might be considered to have been studying and gaining experience for my after career all my life.

Most students, however, are not so fortunately situated, and for them I cannot urge too strongly the necessity of giving ample time to their studies if they hope to make the best of their powers and to establish their art on a firm foundation.

One can hardly write differently as to the period of training for the amateur than for the professional. If Patti said that she was still learning when she had retired from professional singing, no amateur can hope ever to have learned all there is to be known about the art of singing. And since he will always be a lover of song he will always be anxious to learn.

CHAPTER V

QUALITIES NEEDED

NEXT comes the question: What are the qualities which the vocal aspirant, professional or amateur, should possess?

A famous teacher who was once asked this question made answer: "Voice! Voice! Voice!" I agree, and in the case of the professional I should be inclined to add also: "Work! Work! Work!" and then Faith, Hope, and Charity. Without hard work nothing can be done, and the practice of these three virtues will undoubtedly prevent one growing weary in his effort to attain the highest success.

But the truth is, of course, that many other qualities besides voice and industry are necessary here. There are, indeed, so many that I hardly know which to name first.

Lamperti on this point used to say: "First there must be a voice and good ear, but also an artistic soul and a musical disposition." Further, he used to insist upon sound judgment, deep conscientiousness in study, and untiring industry.

Very necessary also are general intelligence and

21

keen perception, because no matter how good a teacher may be the greater part of the work must be done through the brain of the student himself.

On the necessity of sound health it is hardly necessary to insist, while good looks and a fine presence naturally go for much also, though these are not absolutely indispensable, as many notable instances have gone to show.

Then, in addition, there are those temperamental qualities which mean so much: imagination and feeling, sympathy and insight, magnetism and personality. Perhaps, indeed, next to voice and ear these are the most important qualities of all. But unfortunately they cannot be acquired by any amount of study.

How often has it not happened, indeed, that artists have been endowed in all other respects but these! They may have the most beautiful voices, they may sing with the most finished art, but for lack of these incommunicable attributes of the soul they never attain the highest places. They leave their audiences cold because they are cold themselves.

These are artists of the type which Lamperti used to refer to as mere "voice machines"— singers who, as Gounod once put it, are not artists at all in the true sense of the word, but merely people who "play upon the larynx," achieving great results perhaps in the purely vocal and mechanical sense, but never touching the hearts of their hearers for lack of those elemental human qualities which are essential if this result is to be attained.

Let the student do all in his power, therefore, to develop the higher side of his nature. By the study of literature and art, by the reading of fine poetry, by going to good plays, and in every other way let him cultivate his imagination and give play to his finer sensibilities.

For though such qualities as I have referred to may not be acquired when they are non-existent, they may be drawn out and developed if they are merely latent; and in the case of members of the northern races especially this is not infrequently the case.

Another quality of a different kind which is none the less very valuable, indeed essential, is the power of self-criticism; and I attach great importance also to having abundant faith in oneself. Even if it be pushed to the point of vanity and conceit—as I am afraid it occasionally is—this helps enormously when it is a case of withstanding the jolts and jars almost inseparable from the practice of vocal art.

CHAPTER VI

GENERAL CULTURE

OF course, too, wide general culture is very
necessary. Everything that can be possibly
acquired in this way helps, and is, indeed, almost
more necessary to the singer than in the case of
any other branch of the profession.

For the art of the singer is brought into immediate relation with all the other arts. The
singer has to deal with poetry and literature and
the drama—if he takes up opera—in a way quite
unknown to the mere instrumentalist.

A man might be a great pianist or a fine violinist—he might even be a great composer—without ever concerning himself at all with the other
arts. But in the case of the singer this would be
quite impossible.

For it is the singer's business to interpret poetry
in song and to play his part in drama on the stage,
and it is obvious that he cannot hope to do these
things properly without making himself acquainted
with those arts also in addition to his own.

How can one hope, for instance, for a fine interpretation of a great song if the words them-

selves mean nothing to the singer? He may sing the notes, but he cannot possibly do justice to his task unless he enters completely into the spirit of the words and the meaning of the poet.

And in the same way how can one hope to give a satisfactory impersonation of a part in an opera except by studying carefully the drama as a whole, grasping the intentions of the author, making oneself acquainted with the period of the action, and generally entering into it and all the literary, dramatic, historical, and other details of the work as well as considering it from the purely musical point of view?

I am well aware that the opposite practice has often enough been followed. I have heard, indeed, of artists who have sung in such an opera as "Il Trovatore" for years without having ever troubled to understand the course of the action as a whole, and who were consequently in a state of total ignorance as to what it was all about.

But I cannot believe that any one who addressed himself to his task in that unintelligent spirit would ever be likely to give an interpretation of his own part of much significance or value.

In my own case I go so far as to study not only, as a whole, any opera in which I have to take part, but even to learn, or at all events familiarise myself with, all of the other rôles. And I may add that I have found the practice helpful not only to myself but also to my fellow-artists before now, when perhaps some nervous tenor or timid débutante has temporarily "dried up," and I have been enabled to come to the rescue and relieve the situation. This, however, merely *en passant*.

The main point I am insisting on for the moment is that the vocalist who wishes to make the most of his powers cannot have too solid a foundation in the way of general knowledge and culture. There may be no direct connection between the one thing and the other, but his art will benefit none the less—will gain in depth and force and subtlety—in virtue of the fact that it is the outcome of a cultivated nature and the product of a mind which has thought and pondered over the deeper problems of existence.

Chapter VII

STUDY AN INSTRUMENT

I MAY add, too, that there is no excuse for singers to neglect the cultivation of their minds, inasmuch as they have so much more time for this purpose than many of their fellow-students in other branches of the profession.

Thus, while a pianist or a violinist can, and indeed must, practise many hours a day, a singer cannot and should not do this, and therefore they have so much the more time available for the purpose of other study, including, I need hardly say, not only art and literature, but also the other branches of musical culture.

I know that singers have often been reproached in this matter and, I am afraid, not without good reason in earlier days, but I trust and believe that that time is passing away, and that vocalists nowadays are no longer looked upon as being necessarily lacking in general musical knowledge.

To which I need hardly add that many instances could be quoted of famous singers who are or have been admirably equipped also in other respects. The late Madame Sembrich was, for instance, a brilliant all-round musician who played both the piano and the violin with the ability of a professional. Madame Lilli Lehmann, still happily with us, although now advanced in years, is another whose accomplished art was based on fine general musicianship.

In point of fact the vocal student can hardly be too well equipped in the musical sense. He cannot hear too much good instrumental music; he cannot be too well acquainted with the works of the great masters; and, in short, cannot have too wide a basis of general musical knowledge as a foundation for his own specialised branch of the art.

To this end the study of an instrument is, of course, invaluable. The violin is an excellent instrument, though not so helpful from a vocal point of view as the piano. The piano naturally suggests itself as the most useful one for the purpose, since it helps directly in the pupil's vocal studies and makes him independent to some extent of an accompanist. It also gives every facility for obtaining a thorough knowledge of harmony.

It should be employed to further the service of general musical study on the lines above suggested.

Nor should the musical training of the vocalist stop at playing the piano, for he should know something of composition and general theory. A musical education is, indeed, almost indispensable to the singer of the present day if he is to deal successfully with difficult modern music.

In short, the days have gone by when a singer's accomplishments were summed up in the familiar formula of *"Vox et praeterea nihil,"* and he, or she, who expects to achieve a place in the front ranks at the present time must be prepared to use brains as well as vocal cords.

Chapter VIII

VOICE

NEXT comes the question of voice. That this is a fundamental requisite you will not expect me to tell you, although it may be noted, in passing, that some of the greatest singers have started comparatively ill-equipped in this respect —or apparently so.

Of Pasta, for instance, we read that her voice at the outset was heavy and strong, but unequal and very hard to manage. It is said, indeed, that she never to the end of her career succeeded in producing certain notes without some difficulty.

Yet, as the result of incessant study and practice, sometimes pursued in retirement for long periods, she gradually subdued her rebellious and intractable organ, and was eventually recognised as one of the very greatest singers of her time. Jenny Lind's voice at the outset was also very unmanageable.

I might even quote the case of Caruso himself as another example. Caruso was one of my greatest friends. But he gave little promise in his younger days of the wonderful career which was in store for him.

Thus we are told that among his fellow-students at the Scuola Vergina he was known as *"Il tenore vento,"* meaning a thin reedy tenor, and when he had completed his studies neither his master nor any one else had any expectation that he was going to do anything out of the way.

Vergine even remarked humorously of him that if there was any gold in his voice it could only be likened to that at the bottom of the Tiber, inasmuch as it was not worth drawing out. Little did he guess in those days how much rich gold his unpromising pupil was destined to draw in time out of his wonderful organ!

Nor did his earliest appearances impress outside critics any more favourably. The general opinion was that his voice was sympathetic in quality but rather small, and that he himself was lacking in temperament. Caruso lacking in temperament! How odd it seems to us who knew him later! But that was the impression which he produced at first.

All of which goes to show that it is not always easy to say in the beginning how any given voice will turn out in the end.

At the same time I do not wish to encourage the belief that one should begin with a poor voice, or that every mediocre student can hope, with study, to become a Caruso. For this would certainly be a disastrous notion to disseminate.

Such cases as Caruso's are indeed quite exceptional, and in the ordinary way a pupil can take it that if his voice shows no promise at the outset he is not likely to do very much with it later.

On the other hand, what does happen only too frequently, as I have suggested before, is that a pupil starts with a fine voice which, however, through faulty training, want of application, or some other cause, eventually comes to nothing; and it is this which is to be most carefully guarded against.

Sad, it is, indeed, to think of the fine voices which have been lost to the world in this way! Nor need one look very far for instances. Hardly a day passes, indeed, but what one reads or hears of some wonderful voice which has been "discovered" in this place or that. Alas! how few of these wonderful voices eventually justify the hopes which they have aroused! Either the other necessary qualities are lacking, or—too often, I am afraid—their training is entrusted to the wrong hands and they come to nothing.

CHAPTER IX

GOOD AND BAD "MAESTRI"

AS to the absolute necessity of a teacher there can, I suppose, hardly be two opinions. Much can be learnt from books, no doubt; by listening to other singers; and by working things out for oneself, so far as possible. Also it is a fact, doubtless, that some of the world's greatest singers have had remarkably little formal instruction.

Mario, for instance, never had a lesson in his life except when Meyerbeer taught him the part of Raymond in "Robert le Diable"—and Meyerbeer, it is hardly necessary to say, was not a singing master.

But such cases are the exceptions, and in the ordinary way there cannot be the slightest doubt that the services of a teacher are absolutely essential to sound progress. There are exceptions, of course. One of these is the great Chaliapine, who represents his own school and has never had any instruction as we understand it. He is by nature endowed with a beautiful voice, and obtains his fine effects by long hours of deep thought and reflection. I have asked him when and how he prepared, and he replied: "I think out my work in the silence of my bedchamber, when I am waiting for sleep, or in the mornings before I rise. In fact, during all my hours of wakefulness I am always visualising the stage, the actors, the audiences, and contriving how best to obtain effects emotional, sentimental, dramatic."

Grave indeed are the risks run by any student who attempts to supply his own requirements in this matter and to dispense with the skilled advice which only the trained expert can supply—entailing possibly the ruin of his entire career.

It was for lack of such advice in her earlier days that Jenny Lind's voice was almost ruined at the outset, so that when she went to García for advice his verdict was: "It is quite useless for me to think of teaching you, since you have no voice left."

Fortunately rest and proper training saved the situation in that case, as we all know, but how easily it might have been otherwise. Other fine voices have, indeed, been irretrievably destroyed by faulty methods continued too long.

A famous case was that of Duprez, a well-known tenor who flourished some seventy or eighty years ago. "I have lost my voice," he wrote in despair to Rubini, "how have you kept yours?" Rubini replied: "My dear Duprez, you have lost your voice because you have sung with your capital; I have kept mine because I have sung only with the interest." And there is a world of instruction in this pithy way of putting it.

See to it at all costs, therefore, that you put yourself in the right hands. By which I do not necessarily mean a teacher of world-wide repute —for there are many equally good who do not happen to be so generally known. The supremely important thing is that whoever you go to shall be a man—or a woman, as the case may be—of honour and integrity, who can be trusted to deal faithfully with you, and not a quack or a charlatan.

The teaching of singing is indeed a much simpler matter—though difficult enough—than is commonly supposed, especially nowadays when, as the result of scientific study and research, the underlying physiological principles are so much more thoroughly understood than formerly. Yet there will always be those, I suppose, who find it to their advantage to deal with it as something mysterious and occult; and apparently there will always be those confiding souls willing to take these folk at their own valuation and to put good money into their pockets.

Wonderful indeed are the tales which are told of some of these gentry. In New York, for instance, there is said to be a practitioner of this type who sells to his pupils, in order to give timbre to their voices, bottles (at two dollars each) of Italian water. Beware of the confidence tricksters of the musical profession who claim to transform your voice by some quack method or theory of "nasal resonance" and so on. These people have ruined more voices than one could enumerate.

But one need not go to America to find examples. I am afraid, indeed, that even in my own native land the same sort of thing is not entirely unknown. I have even heard of a teacher in Milan who makes his pupils swear on a crucifix not to reveal the secret of his wonderful "method," and I have heard of another whose practice it was to make his pupils tie to the legs of the piano pieces of elastic which they were instructed to pull out and let go again, in order to "feel" the gradations of *crescendo* and *diminuendo*.

But even he seems to have been excelled in invention by another "Professor"—again hailing from the Land of the Stars and Stripes!—whose custom it was to illustrate the art of *mezza voce* by means of an umbrella which he opened and closed as his happy pupils, standing before him, swelled and diminished on the chosen note.

Such things, you may say, sound laughable enough, but they are no laughing matter for the unfortunate pupils who happen to be the victims of such monstrous quackery, and I cannot urge too earnestly upon all my readers the supreme importance of choosing a teacher who is above all suspicion—for preference one possessed of a satisfactory diploma obtained at a recognised institution.

Then you may be sure that whether the teacher be better or worse in the purely technical sense, he will at least be an honest man and not one who makes his calling a mere pretext for the plundering of the ignorant and unwary.

Another important question which arises in this connection is as to the advisability of studying at home or abroad, and this, I am afraid, is one of those perplexing matters in the case of which there is a good deal to be said on both sides. I myself have naturally a prejudice in favour of my beloved Italy, the traditional Land of Song, where, I am proud to think, the art of Bel Canto still finds its finest exponents and teachers, and where also there are greater facilities, I suppose, for hearing fine singing than in any other country in the world.

At the same time I am quite prepared to admit that there is a good deal to be said on the other side. It is a great undertaking and responsibility, for instance, sending a young girl to study abroad. The teacher selected may not be a good one, or may not be suited to her particular requirements, when she gets there—although by saying this I do not mcan to express agreement with those who contend that a special kind of teaching is required for the singers of every nationality. Whether you study at home or abroad, let your teacher be the best you can obtain.

CHAPTER X

COMPASS AND QUALITY

HAVING found your teacher, the next thing you will want to know is precisely what sort of voice you have—and this is a matter, curiously enough, which cannot always be determined offhand. The strangest mistakes have, indeed, not infrequently been made in this respect—as in the well-known instance of Jean de Reszke, who actually began his public career as a baritone and continued singing for some years before he finally came to the conclusion that his voice was, in reality, a tenor.

The important task of discovering whether a voice is bass, baritone, tenor, contralto, mezzo-soprano, or soprano, and the exact character of the general ranges of these voices is a matter of great delicacy, and cannot be decided at one hearing. It is largely individual, and sometimes a matter of health and circumstances. The ranges of different classes of the human voice may be generally stated as follows. In the bass voice two octaves of E, the contralto two octaves of E with a tone and a half more in the upper notes leading

39

to G; the tenor, which sounds an octave lower than the soprano, and the soprano voice itself two octaves of C.   There are also the baritone and mezzo-soprano voices, the former of which is neither bass nor tenor, and the latter neither contralto nor soprano.   The average range covers two octaves of G or A in baritones and mezzo-sopranos.

In all cases there are, of course, exceptions, as, for example, the bass that extends to a melodious low C and can even reach the baritone top F. There is a further classification which has relation to the *timbre,* or colour, which distinguishes whether the artist is dramatic or purely lyric.   If of a lyric tendency the artist will do well to avoid dramatic declamation until maturity and experience has taught him this difficult side of our art and *vice versa.*

It is not a question of compass only, but of compass in addition to the distinctive character and quality of the voice.   But compass is undoubtedly essential, and in regard to this Lamperti's practice was to judge not only by the notes which could be taken, but by the facility with which words could be enunciated on them at the same time.

Thus, in the case of a girl student, if she could not only sing the upper G, but could also enunciate words easily on that note, he considered that she was a true soprano; and so on with all the other voices. Thus a baritone might be able to take notes almost as high as a tenor. But if he could not pronounce words comfortably on those notes he was not, in Lamperti's judgment, to be classed as anything but a baritone.

But, as a general rule, your teacher will not have much difficulty in deciding as to the classification of your voice, and, presuming this to have been decided, we must consider next the question of training it.

Here I feel that I must go carefully, for if there is one thing more certain than another, in my opinion, it is that the pupil who hopes to get the best results from his training must place himself unreservedly in his teacher's hands, since otherwise he cannot possibly hope to do justice to his teaching. That is to say, he should not confuse his mind by accepting the advice and instruction of other people—so far, at all events, as concerns what may be called the strictly technical side of his training.

Therefore, I shall confine myself to general hints and observations only, based on my own experiences and herewith offered for what they are worth.

Chapter XI

AGE TO START TRAINING

AS to the age to start training the voice, this depends to some extent upon the individual, but speaking generally it may be said that in the case of boys the voice matures at about the ages of from fourteen to sixteen, and that no serious work should be undertaken until after this period. Although choir-singing for boys affords wonderful training—in some cases, at all events, if not in all —it should not be persisted in too long.

If boys are allowed to sing on in the choir until their voices change, they may easily find, finally, that they have totally ruined their vocal organs for the rest of their lives. The utmost caution should be exercised, therefore, in this matter, and it should be the duty of every choirmaster to see that none of his choristers are permitted to run this grave risk by continuing their services too long.

In the case of girls, teaching may begin about the age of sixteen or seventeen, but not much earlier.

CHAPTER XII

ANATOMY AND PHYSIOLOGY

TO what extent a vocal student should be instructed in matters anatomical and physiological is a question which has often been raised, and upon which the most contradictory views have been expressed. It is argued by some, that having in mind all the great singers of the past who flourished before the laryngoscope was thought of that the less the student knows about such things the better. It is contended that he will surely become self-conscious and unnatural by thinking about the physiological mechanism of processes which should be absolutely instinctive and automatic; and possibly in some instances this does occur.

I do not think, however, that if the instruction is properly given it need have any such effect, and I thoroughly believe, myself, in the student being given at least a general idea as to the construction of the vocal organs and the manner in which they function.

To precisely what extent the student should be instructed in what a famous singer once humorously referred to as "thoracic, crico-thyroideal, and epiglottic matters" may be a question for consideration, but as to the desirability of his being acquainted in a general way with the working of the vocal apparatus I have no sort of doubt.

The truth is that the whole business of singing, if reduced to its elements, is much simpler and easier to understand than is sometimes supposed, and there is not the slightest reason why any difficulty need be experienced in explaining the matter in its general outlines. I would go further, indeed, and say that he is not likely to prove a very intelligent pupil who is not sufficiently curious and interested to wish to know something upon the subject.

At the same time, it is, no doubt, perfectly true that many of the greatest singers of the past have been destitute of the slightest knowledge of such matters. In which connection one may recall the famous saying of Patti when interrogated as to her method: "Je n'en sais rien." But it does not follow that others not possessed of her marvellous natural gifts should follow her example in this respect. For she did unconsciously and instinctively what in the case of most others only comes as the result of laborious study and practice.

One may recall, in this connection, the saying of that profound student of the art on the technical side, who was also in her day such a great executant, Lilli Lehmann, that it is not enough to sing well, one must be told also the how and why, and be given a firm foundation, if permanent results are to be hoped for. For otherwise one will

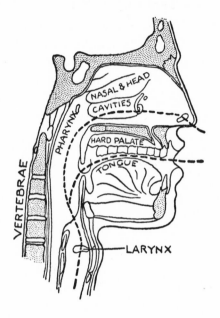

ROUGH SECTION OF NOSE, MOUTH, AND PHARYNX, SUGGESTING BY DOTTED LINES HOW THE TONE PASSES FROM THE LARYNX THROUGH THE MOUTH AND PASSAGES OF THE HEAD.

run the risk of coming to grief when for some reason or other an unexpected strain is put upon one's resources and there is no sound knowledge and understanding to fall back upon.

How can one properly understand, for instance, the all-important subject of breathing, if one has not at least some idea as to the natural processes involved?   Vocal teachers and students of voice production are often twitted upon the conflicting character of the views which they hold and the principles which they lay down, but here is one subject, at all events, upon which there is universal agreement, namely, the supreme importance of right breathing as the very foundation of the singer's art.

CHAPTER XIII

BREATHING

HE who breathes properly sings properly, it
has been said; and there is not a single
authority of any weight, I venture to say, who
does not endorse that statement. The old Italian
masters used to say, indeed, that the art of singing
is the art of breathing; and the same idea was
put by Lamperti in another way when he observed
that "the attainment of proper respiration should
be the first object of the student of singing."

On the same subject the words of a famous
English singing teacher, William Shakespeare,
may be quoted. In his well-known work on the
Art of Song he lays down as the two fundamental
aims to be set before himself by the student: 1,
how to take a breath and how to press it out
slowly; and, 2, how to sing to this controlled
breath pressure.

It is when we come to consider the views of
the different theorists in detail that divergencies
will be found to arise. But on certain fundamental matters there will, I think, be found pretty
general agreement nowadays.

47

The great guiding principle to be borne in mind, in my opinion, is ease and naturalness. This is one of those matters in regard to which nature can be trusted much more safely than theorists and professors. I refer, of course, to the actual process of breathing. As regards the subsequent production of tone there is, of course, plenty to be

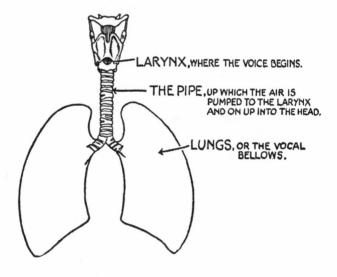

LARYNX, WHERE THE VOICE BEGINS.

THE PIPE, UP WHICH THE AIR IS PUMPED TO THE LARYNX AND ON UP INTO THE HEAD.

LUNGS, OR THE VOCAL BELLOWS.

ROUGH DIAGRAM OF THE LARYNX, TRACHEA AND LUNGS.

taught. But the actual process of inspiration and exhalation should be as natural and as easy as possible.

Some wise words of Salvatore Marchesi may be quoted on this point: "When explaining the physical, mechanical process of breathing to beginners it is essential to make them understand that natural laws have provided for its independence of our will, as is observed in sleeping. Therefore, every intentional preparation or effort made in order to draw more air into the lungs will produce the contrary result, hindering the freedom of the natural process."

But this is not to imply that breathing capacity cannot be cultivated and developed by practice. On the contrary, a vast amount can be done in this way, just as in the case of any other organ of the body, by means of systematic exercise and practice. Everyone has heard, for instance, of the wonderful way in which the breathing capacity of native divers in the tropics is developed in the course of their calling, or of that old man in the Bay of Naples who stops under the water with a watch in hand for 35 seconds. Singers can acquire something of the same power, and must do so, indeed, if they hope ever to achieve the best results. For the production of good sustained tone is impossible if the art of breathing is not properly understood and acquired.

Among modern singers no one attached more importance to breathing and breath control than the late Signor Caruso, and no one, certainly, attained more wonderful results in this way. He developed his powers to such an extent indeed in this respect, that it was said that he could move a grand piano by the expansion of the muscles of his diaphragm! And whether this be true or not it is certain that his wonderful breathing capacity was, as he himself used to declare, in large measure the secret of his consummate art.

Try to avoid breathing through the mouth. Inhalation through the nostrils purifies and warms the air before it reaches the throat. Breathing through the mouth dries the throat and makes the voice husky. Nevertheless, in singing declamatory music what are called half-breaths through the mouth are necessary.

When practising avoid taking sudden breaths, though this may also be necessary when performing publicly.

Practise once daily before a looking-glass and so correct faults of breathing and grimaces.

Don't heave the shoulders when taking breath. There should be no visible movement of the body.

When practising breathing—and this should be done every day—inhale a long slow breath to the full lung capacity, hold for one or two seconds, and then exhaust in the same slow gentle way. This is rather exhausting, and two or three periods of five minutes with an interval of say fifteen minutes should be sufficient for each day.

Chapter XIV

VOCAL CORDS

B UT, of course, breathing alone is not sufficient. After the breathing capacity has been developed the power thus acquired must be rightly applied, and here the first principle is right emission, and in particular the rule that the release of the breath and the attack of the tone must take place simultaneously. In other words, no breath at all must be permitted to escape before the production of tone.

It is to attain this result that the so-called *coup de glotte*, or "shock of the glottis," has been advocated. To appreciate this term it is necessary to understand exactly how vocal tone is produced.

I will not attempt to go into the matter fully, but the general principles involved are quite easily grasped.

Taken broadly, then, it will be understood that vocal sound is produced by a column of air passing from the lungs through a small aperture formed by the vocal cords within the larynx (see diagrams). When we breathe in the ordinary way the air passes in and out as we inspire and exhale, without any sound being produced. This is because the passage through the larynx is then quite clear. No obstruction is offered to the air current, and in consequence the process is quite noiseless.

When, however, we wish to utter a sound, Nature provides for this by enabling us to interpose an obstruction to the air current by means of the vocal cords, and the air then has to pass through a small slit or aperture, sometimes called the

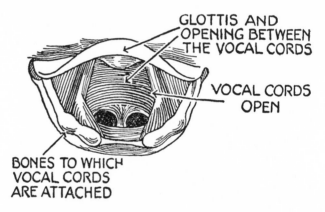

GLOTTIS AND
OPENING BETWEEN
THE VOCAL CORDS

VOCAL CORDS
OPEN

BONES TO WHICH
VOCAL CORDS
ARE ATTACHED

THE VOCAL CORDS DURING DEEP BREATHING.

"vocal chink," formed by their being drawn closely together curtainwise, as it were.

When the vocal cords—or ligaments, as they are perhaps better described—are drawn together in this manner the passage of the air is so restricted that it can only pass in short rapid pulsations, instead of, as before, in a continuous stream, and

the result of these pulses or vibrations is the production of sound or tone.

The aperture, or chink, is called the glottis, and
the character of the tone resulting, in particular
the pitch of it, is regulated by the precise disposition and proximity to one another of the two
bands or cords or ligaments—sometimes they are
known as the vocal lips—by which the chink or
opening is formed.

The process itself of regulating the opening of
the vocal cords in this way is entirely automatic

THE VOCAL CORDS DURING THE SINGING OF A
HIGH NOTE.

and subconscious. We merely *will* to produce a
tone of a certain pitch and the vocal cords automatically, and without any conscious effort on
our part, are brought together to precisely the
right degree necessary to produce that particular
tone.

From this it will be understood that every note

that is uttered, every inflection even of the speaking voice, however minute, requires a slightly different adjustment of these infinitely delicate threadlike membranes which are provided for this purpose within the box-like larynx; and this extraordinarily delicate adjustment is all effected quite automatically and instinctively by the mere operations of the will.

The brain intimates, so to speak, that it requires a certain note to be produced and forthwith, without the slightest conscious act of adjustment on the part of the singer or speaker, the vocal ligaments adapt themselves precisely in the manner required and the particular note desired is duly produced.

And these notes may issue forth through that tiny aperture and from the throat of the singer to the number of a dozen or more in a second— each one requiring a separate adjustment of the aperture and the said adjustment being effected in every instance, in the case of a properly trained singer, absolutely perfectly and exactly.

Surely of all the many wonderful contrivances which go to the making of the mechanism of the human body there is none which is more wonderful than this! It is, indeed, necessary only to consider the elaboration of the means and the complexity of the muscular adjustments necessary to achieve similar results in the case of a violin, say, or a piano, in order to realise the amazing ingenuity and efficiency of the means employed by Nature.

But I am wandering from the *coup de glotte,* which I set out to explain. Let it be understood, therefore, that the *coup de glotte* is merely a name for a particular method of bringing together the lips of the vocal cords and certain subordinate muscles, known as the ventricular bands, with a view to a better and cleaner production of tone, and with a view especially to the avoidance of the particular fault above referred to, namely, the emission of air before the production of the note.

In the result the "attack" is certainly very sharp and clean, but personally I cannot recommend this particular method of achieving that result, since the effect is anything but agreeable to the ear, and there is good reason for thinking that the practice, besides being unnecessary, is also injurious to a vocal organ.

I will not go further into the matter, however, since all such technical details are for the teacher to explain and illustrate and cannot be satisfactorily dealt with in print.

Certain general principles may, however, be touched on, amongst which the first is, perhaps, that there should never be at any time the smallest conscious strain or effort. Relaxation, looseness, ease, should be the watchwords all the time. Rigidity, tightening of the muscles, stiffness, contraction, are fatal to the production of beautiful tone. Here, as so often in art, when grace and beauty are the objects aimed at, economy of effort is the grand secret.

There should never be any strain or forcing of any sort or kind, and on the same principle, it may be noted, is the rule as to the amount of breath emitted, which should always be the smallest quantity possible which suffices to produce the tone required. Let out enough breath and no more—keeping the remainder in reserve—that is one of the fundamental secrets of beautiful tone production.

Lilli Lehmann puts the same point in another way when she insists on the supreme importance of emitting "as little breath as possible." Perhaps I may be permitted to quote, also, in this connection some interesting remarks of Signor Salvatore Fucito, in a recently published volume, in reference to the practice of Caruso in this regard.

"Caruso governed the expiratory flow of the breath with such mastery that not a particle of it escaped without giving up its necessary equivalent in tone. Caruso emitted for each musical phrase, or for each note, just enough breath to produce that phrase or note musically and *no more*. The remaining breath he kept in reserve, which made the enchanted hearer feel that the master was still far from the limit of his resources, that he had still ample motive power in reserve for whatever the occasion might require."

Another great master of breathing is Battistini. One hears him singing long phrases, one after the other, without perceiving when or how he fills his lungs, so completely has he covered up all traces of the physical effort. There is no puffing and panting, no discoloration or distortion of the face.

I am myself often asked how I manage to find the breath for the long florid passages which I so often have to sing, and my reply usually is that I have a good pair of bellows which I make a point of always keeping well filled with air.

This can be done, I may add, in the case of such passages as I have mentioned by taking at times only partial breaths instead of full ones. These can naturally be taken much more quickly than complete inspirations, and by their means the "bellows" can be kept constantly replenished even when the heaviest demands are being made upon their contents.

But while it is essential to maintain a good pressure of air behind the tone, this does not mean that the lungs must be filled to distention, for this produces the worst possible result. Madame Lilli Lehmann has recorded, for instance, in her valuable treatise on singing, that she made this mistake in the first instance, with the result that she always felt as if she must release some of her superfluous breath before beginning to sing.

"Undoubtedly," she writes, "I took in too much air in breathing and cramped various muscles, thereby depriving my breathing organs and muscles of their elasticity. I often had, with all my care and preparation for inhalation, too little breath, and sometimes, when not giving special thought to it, more than enough." And others not infrequently commit the same error under the mistaken impression that they must get as much air into their lungs as possible.

CHAPTER XV

PLACING THE VOICE

A N all-important part of the student's training is that in relation to what is called the "placing" of the voice. This somewhat vague term has been the subject of a good deal of misunderstanding, and the most curious notions have gained currency as to its actual meaning. Yet this is, in reality, quite simple.

Tone is made in the first instance, as I have already explained, by the breath passing through the vocal cords. The precise *quality* of the tone depends, however, on the formation and disposition of the various parts of the vocal apparatus—throat, palate, tongue, and so on—through which the breath afterwards passes before issuing from the mouth.

The disposition of these various parts can be varied by the individual, and the placing of the voice consists in finding how best to adjust them in order to get the most satisfactory tone, and in acquiring the power always to produce tone in this way and in no other.

To assist in attaining this result it is usual to

instruct the pupil to sing "forward," "dans le masque," and so on, but it should be clearly understood that though such terms are useful from the practical point of view, they are none the less only a *façon de parler,* and a means of instructing the pupil how to adjust and adapt the whole vocal apparatus, so to speak, in the most effective way.

You can really produce a tone in your face or in your throat. It is all produced by the vocal cords, and nowhere else, and merely receives its specific quality or character, so to speak, by, in part, the natural formation, and, in part, the conscious adjustment of the passages through which it passes on its way to the mouth.

But by thinking of the face or the throat and, so to speak, *apparently* fixing it there, you can modify the disposition of the various parts in question and so influence the quality of the tone produced. This mysterious placing of the voice means, therefore, in reality, nothing more than finding out in each individual instance the best position of the vocal organs for getting the best results.

This, again, is one of those matters in regard to which little help can be derived from advice in books. Only by direct instruction from a capable master can a pupil possibly be made to understand completely what is required in this respect.

It is, indeed, essentially one of those matters in the case of which an ounce of practice and example is worth a ton of theory, and happy is the student who has the good fortune to go to a master capable of instructing him rightly on the point.

Some fortunate ones, like myself, have voices which are quite perfectly placed by Nature. That is to say, they are the lucky possessors of voices which they produce naturally and unconsciously in the most advantageous manner, so that they require to make no alteration at all.

This will, of course, be perceived at once by a capable master, who will be only too careful in such cases to leave well enough alone. A charlatan or impostor, on the other hand, can work irremediable harm by interfering with such voices and attempting to modify or improve them.

A singer with a perfect light soprano voice may, for instance, have the misfortune to fall into the hands of such a teacher, who will persuade her that she can sing the rôles of a dramatic soprano, and by misguided advice and training succeed in ruining a beautiful natural voice in the attempt to improve it.

In the vast majority of cases, however, the pupil's voice is not naturally placed so as to give the best results. That is to say, by proper instruction and training it can be made to produce better results—tones more smooth, more round, more resonant, and so on—and it is here that the services of an experienced and capable teacher are beyond price. The problem is one of great complexity, for so many different factors enter into it. The palate, the tongue, the teeth, the lips, as well as the natural and unalterable formation of the throat, and so forth, all play their part in determining the issue, and the slightest modifications in anyone may easily effect the greatest differences in the results.

It is easy to understand, therefore, how impossible it is to lay down any general rules in the matter, but it is perhaps safe to say that the less the pupil is called upon to depart from his, or her, natural and instinctive procedure, the more likely are good results to be achieved—the ideal case being, of course, the one in which no alterations whatsoever are required.

I may add, perhaps, that some authorities attach great importance in this connection to the language used by the pupil in the earlier stages of his training—that is, when his voice is undergoing the process of being placed. That accomplished singer Signor Bonci is, for instance, one who holds strong views on this point.

According to him it is very injurious for singers at this stage of their studies to sing in more than one language. I may perhaps venture to quote what he has written on the subject: "When a tone is properly placed the word need not affect it, but a great deal of harm is caused by applying the word too early and beyond this by using several languages. It is a question, and a serious one, whether those who teach singing understand the application of the word to the tone, and the dangers are obvious in languages where nasals and gutturals prevail."

Chapter XVI

REGISTERS

CLOSELY allied with the question of "placing" is that of "registers," which has been the subject of so much controversy at various times. There is not even agreement as to how many registers there are—or even if there are any at all.

For while some take the view that there are no such things, others speak variously of two, three, four, and even more natural and inevitable divisions in the range of the average voice which can only be properly distinguished from one another in this way.

Some, I believe, even maintain that each individual note should properly be regarded as a different register. But this suggestion I think can scarcely be intended seriously. For if each individual note really does constitute a separate register, what is gained by talking of registers at all?

There is, however, no denying that there are certain marked differences in the case of every voice in the quality of the tone produced at different parts of its range or compass—differences of tone quality which are accompanied also by different sensations on the part of the singer; and to these different sections of the vocal range the name of registers has been given.

Usually three are recognised—chest, medium, and head, the term chest register being applied to the lowest notes, medium to the middle portion, and head to the highest.

The terms chest, medium, and head are derived from the sensations experienced by the singer in producing the different notes referred to—the lower ones giving the feeling of having been produced in the chest, the middle ones in the throat, and the highest ones of all in the head. But it should be understood that in actual fact there is no difference in the manner in which the various notes are produced.

All the notes of the voice, whether high or low, are in reality produced in the same way, namely, in the manner already described—by the passage of the air from the lungs through the "chink" formed by the vocal cords. In the case of the lower notes, however, owing to certain physiological causes, the vibrations are felt by the singer most strongly in and about the chest, and in the case of the higher ones in the head—whence, therefore, the somewhat misleading terms in use have been adopted.

At the same time the fact that these different

sensations are experienced by the singer may be taken as the best possible evidence of the fact that there are definite differences in the method of tone production to account for them; and this view of the matter is in fact confirmed by the researches of physiologists.

There is no need, of course, for vocalists to concern themselves with the matter in detail, for the process involved is, of course, entirely (or almost entirely) automatic. But it is none the less explained by the physiologists quite clearly why there is, at a certain point, this difference of feeling on the part of the singer in passing from the lower notes to the higher ones.

Without going too minutely into the matter, the reason broadly stated is that the vocal cords are differently disposed in the two cases. Up to a certain point the successive tones are produced in one uniform way, and then above that point the method is modified; and it is this difference accordingly which is accountable for the distinctive sensations experienced by the singer—sensations, it may be added, which have been recognised and discussed ever since the art of singing has been studied.

Hence, it is quite a mistake to suggest, as has been done by some, that the whole notion of registers is a delusion. These different registers do undoubtedly exist, and it becomes one of the most important problems consequently to get rid of the "break," or change in the tone quality, which occurs when the voice passes from one to the other. At the same time it does not follow that violent and artificial methods should be adopted for this purpose.

On the contrary, little else than steady and properly directed practice is required in the ordinary way to accomplish this. In fact if you get your breathing right and your tone production in general right, the register difficulty will probably solve itself. To put it in another way, if you ensure that each individual tone is right, the problem of the registers need not seriously trouble you; and this is a matter of paying attention to the general rules of sound tone production.

Special exercises are, however, usually given for the purpose of "equalising" the voice, as it is called, that is to say, for the purpose of ensuring a perfectly even and uniform quality of tone throughout the scale and avoiding the break at the change of register which has been referred to; and these exercises are no doubt useful.

Most of the best authorities are agreed that proper breathing has as much to do with the matter as anything, some even going so far as to say that the matter should not be mentioned to the student at all. This is perhaps a somewhat extreme statement, but the underlying principle

is sound.   And here, as always, the principle of
absolute ease and relaxation and the avoidance of
all unnatural muscular contraction or violent effort
is at once all important.

The following is generally conceded to be a well-

thought-out method of uniting the voice wherever
the "break" occurs.

Sing this passage *Messa di Voce* ascending and
descending, commencing where the break is first
noticeable.   If this is practised consistently for two
or three periods of twenty minutes a day it should
be effective in preventing this unpleasant defect.
Begin firmly, using "ay," "oh," or "ee," and swell
out to fullest capacity.   Then let the tone die
away imperceptibly and be careful not to use
falsetto.   By doing the foregoing we have augmented the head tones to such an extent that instead of having falsetto, we have a head voice
capable of being allied to the chest voice with
practically no distinguishable break in the whole
compass.

Contraltos are the greatest sinners with the
"break."   Very few contraltos are able to change
the registers or sing two octaves without a perceptible gap.   At one time this vulgar habit was

considered a virtue when in reality it is a clear indication of lack of study and practice.

Remember that no matter where the "break" occurs it is only by cultivating the head voice that a cure can be attained.

Then, again, almost everybody has one or two tones more or less defective, and wherever these occur special attention must be given them so that they can be built up until the singer can safely overcome the "break."

CHAPTER XVII

FAULTS

A FEW words on faults—and the correction of them. No, I am not going to attempt a catalogue of all the faults which are possible, but name just a few: faulty intonation; faulty phrasing; imperfectly attacking notes; "scooping" up to notes; "digging" or arriving at a note from a semitone beneath it; singing off the key or out of tune and tremolo. All of these faults are unforgivable, but the last two are crimes. And I could name numbers more. I have heard vocalists who have been horrified when I told them that they arrived at a note after attacking it from a fourth below, especially when singing *pianissimo*. Consequently I cannot over-emphasise the supreme need for the student to recognise his faults and follies if he hopes ever to make progress.

Nay, this is not putting it strongly enough. He should not merely be ready to recognise his faults, but eager to discover them. He should be ever on the lookout to realise his deficiencies and to regard as his best friends those who are kind enough to tell him of them.

This may sound self-obvious, but I am afraid that in practice the attitude of the average student —and not of the student only, but also of the experienced artist—is very different. A fatal self-satisfaction seems, for some reason or other, to be one of the commonest failings of the average singer. One fairly well-known singer invited my criticism of her voice, and when I obliged and told her what she must do to become a great artist she replied, "But I am a great artist." At which I bowed and said, "I beg your pardon, madam."

Yet it is hardly necessary to say—we can all realise it indeed in the case of others—that there is no form of weakness more absolutely fatal to artistic progress. Let the student beware, therefore, of this dangerous form of vanity and self-sufficiency, and learn from all who can teach him.

How often have I not heard of students—alike young and old—who have been foolish enough to throw over good teachers because they have been honest enough and courageous enough to tell them unpalatable truths! They think they know better. They are so supremely well pleased with themselves—so foolishly satisfied with their own achievements—that they regard it as an offence when their errors are pointed out.

Of course they do not put it—even to themselves —in this way. They prefer to persuade themselves that their teacher is at fault. They explain that they do not like his "method." Or they say that he does not "understand" their particular voice. And so they come to the conclusion that they had better make a change and go to some other master instead.

It is all very human but very foolish, and I cannot impress this too strongly upon all who read this book. Your best friend is one who will tell you faithfully, not how beautifully you sing but how badly!

Some are, of course, wise enough to realise this. And you will generally find that they are the ones who get on. Such a one was Caruso, who, to the end of his day, never ceased to practise, to study, to reflect upon his art, and even to worry and agitate himself over his supposed deficiencies—deficiencies which were unperceived by his hearers but which he, with his fastidious and ultra-sensitive artistic conscience, persuaded himself were there.

Chapter XVIII

COLORATURA SINGING

I SUPPOSE there is no question which I am more frequently asked by vocal students and others interested than how to acquire agility, but I am afraid my answer is usually disappointing. For I can only repeat that it is simply a case of perseverance and hard work, plus, of course, whatever natural abilities in that direction you may possess.

It is obvious that all singers are not equally endowed in this respect. The mere fact that there is such a difference in this matter between the various classes of voices is sufficient to prove that. No one ever expects a contralto voice to have the same facility in this regard as a light soprano, and still less a bass or a baritone.

The most unceasing practice would never have enabled an Alboni or a Lablache, say, to achieve the dazzling runs and fioriture of a Patti or a Catalani. And to a less marked degree there are similar differences between individual voices of the same class. All are not equally capable in this particular even when in other respects they may be equally good.

Some experienced teachers indeed recognise this fact so clearly that they do not advise even soprano singers to cultivate coloratura singing unless they have the necessary natural facility to begin with. I think myself, however, that all should endeavour to acquire the maximum agility, even if they do not attempt to sing coloratura in public, simply for the benefits which they will derive from it in other respects. After all the voice cannot be possessed of too much flexibility whatever style of music be attempted; and there is no way in which flexibility can be more surely developed than by the practice of coloratura.

For the rest I can only repeat that, given the right kind of voice in the first place, there is only one way to acquire agility, and that is by practice. No short cuts are possible here, and I have no trade secrets to impart.

And the necessary exercises themselves are all of the simplest character, at all events in the beginning; just simple scales—or rather portions of scales—in the first instance, with others more elaborate in due course. But the scales are the foundation, and if they are properly mastered the rest will follow without difficulty.

An important feature of good coloratura singing is, of course, not only that the notes shall be cleanly sung, but also that they shall be absolutely in tune and of good tone quality. One not infrequently hears singers who possess the necessary agility to sing the note, but are lacking in these other qualities. Their runs will lack brilliancy because the notes will not be perfectly in tune, and the quality of them will be so hard and disagreeable sometimes as to give more pain than pleasure.

The cause of this will usually have been a desire to make progress too hastily in the earlier stages. They will not have devoted sufficient attention at the outset to practising *slowly,* and so ensuring absolutely just intonation and satisfactory tone quality. Therefore, it is emphatically a case here of "more haste less speed." You cannot acquire velocity quickly. I will not repeat again the well-worn story of Porpora and Caffarelli. But that illustrates the point.

I cannot refrain from adding a few words while on this subject in defence of coloratura, which is so often contemptuously spoken of in these days by those who do not possess the power of singing it. We all know the kind of way in which it is referred to. Coloratura music is false, showy, superficial, unworthy, dramatically unreal, and so on. But what nonsense this is!

What is the difference in principle, I would ask, between the fioriture passages of the vocalist and those introduced as a matter of course in the most serious instrumental music? Why should a cadenza for the voice be reckoned less worthy than a similar passage for the violin or the 'cello? All the greatest masters have introduced florid passages in plenty in the noblest instrumental music. Yet the view is very generally adopted that these are inadmissible, or, at all events, belong to an inferior phase of the art when the instrument employed happens to be the voice.

No doubt the quality of the works more particularly identified with vocal music of this order has had something to do with the matter. Yet it is hardly necessary to recall that vocal fioriture is by no means confined to the music of Donizetti, Bellini, and the like.

Bach, for one, had no sort of prejudice on the point, as is demonstrated often enough even in his most solemn work, while Handel, again, revelled in coloratura, alike in the case of his operas, containing some of the most wonderful florid music ever written, and of his oratorios, to which no less applied.

That Mozart can be reckoned in the same category it is hardly necessary to recall, while even Beethoven did not disdain to utilise the arts of vocal decoration in many of the numbers of "Fidelio." If, therefore, coloratura singing is sometimes spoken of disrespectfully, it is not from

lack of distinguished names which can be cited in
its defence.

Nor is it only among the ancients that such are
to be found.   In the modern Russian School we
have Rimsky-Kosakoff's "Hymn to the Sun" from
"Coq d'Or."   And have we not also such an
eminently serious master as Richard Strauss chal-
lenging comparison in our own time with the most
extravagant productions of the past in this particular genre in the music of Zerbinetta in his
"Ariadne"?   One of his latest songs, "Amor," is
purely for coloratura singers.

As to the charge that coloratura in dramatic
music is unnatural and undramatic, those who
argue thus surely overlook the fact that all opera
might with equal justice be disposed of in the
same manner.   People do not express themselves
in song in real life, any more than they speak in
blank verse, as they are made to do in Shake-
spearean drama.

Yet we are glad to have "Don Giovanni" and
"King Lear" none the less!   It is, indeed, truly
straining at a gnat and swallowing a camel to condemn coloratura while accepting opera as a whole.

I go further than this, for I venture to say that
coloratura can be not only delightful to the ear
but also thoroughly appropriate and dramatically
expressive.   What could be more suitable to give

expression to the madness of Lucia than the roulades which Donizetti gives to her? Or how could the joy of Marguérite be more exquisitely expressed than in the strains of Gounod's "Jewel Song"?

I might point in this connection, did modesty permit it, to what people have been good enough to say concerning my own treatment of coloratura in "La Traviata" and elsewhere. I recall that when I first appeared in London it was upon this point particularly that all my critics dwelt.

They were all more especially struck by the manner in which I managed, while singing Verdi's florid music brilliantly and effectively in the purely vocal sense, at the same time to make it expressive; and this I took as the greatest possible compliment which could be bestowed on me. For that I think is what coloratura properly sung should be.

It should please the ear by its brilliance, but at the same time it should not, and need not, obscure the dramatic significance of what is sung. I might on this point quote that great artist once again, Lilli Lehmann, who, notwithstanding her strong leaning to music of the more serious class, including Wagner, in which she was so wonderful, was yet a great coloratura singer herself in her younger days, and who has strongly insisted upon the possibility of making even the most florid music expressive also when it is sung in the right way.

She writes: "Thus in the coloratura passages of Mozart's arias I have always sought to gain expressiveness by *crescendi*, choice of significant points for breathing, and breaking off of phrases. I have been especially successful with this in the 'Entführung,' introducing a tone of lament in the first aria, a heroic dignity into the second, through the coloratura passages."

But happily I do not think there is any likelihood of coloratura ever going out of fashion, whatever its detractors may say, so long, at all events, as singers shall be forthcoming who are capable of responding to its demands.

CHAPTER XIX

ENUNCIATION

AFTER the fundamental problems of breathing, tone production and so forth have been dealt with, there is nothing to which the student should pay greater attention than the question of diction, or right enunciation. Yet I am afraid it is rare to find that this view of the matter is acted upon. On the contrary, this question of diction appears to be one of the last to which most singers are disposed to give any serious attention.

Hence the unintelligible sounds which are so often heard proceeding from vocalists, alike in the concert room and on the stage, so that one sometimes can scarcely tell even in what language they are supposed to be singing.

This is, of course, a deplorable state of affairs, but yet one so well established that in nine cases out of ten it is hardly thought worthy of remark by the average hearer. It is taken as a matter of course, in other words, that only a word or two, here and there, of those sung shall be understood by the audience, and one may listen attentively to an entire opera without having more than a vague idea at the end as to what it was all about.

Yet in the case of certain singers one may understand without difficulty practically every word they sing, the fact being thereby demonstrated that there is not the slightest real necessity for the incredibly slovenly and defective enunciation which is permitted with such surprising and lamentable tolerance by the public at large.

So far as opera is concerned, I think that the blame rests largely with the managers. If they would adopt the practice of deputing some trustworthy representative at every rehearsal to sit in the topmost gallery and relentlessly pull up every singer whose words could not be clearly understood, the difficulty, I am convinced, would speedily disappear. And operatic directors, I am sure, would find it greatly to their advantage to adopt this course if only on account of the greater popularity which opera would enjoy if it could always be followed, as it should be, as easily as a spoken play.

I believe that in England especially, where opera in the native language is, as I am delighted to see, making such steady headway, its acceptance by the general public is hindered more on this account than by any other reason. Yet there is not the slightest necessity for the presentation of the drama, which is sung instead of being spoken, to be hampered and handicapped in this grievous fashion, and it only needs more vigorous action on the part of the directing powers, I am persuaded, to remedy matters.

So long, however, as singers are left to themselves in this respect, the difficulty will always remain, since their inevitable tendency is to sacrifice diction to tone quality—in other words, to achieve the best effects in the purely vocal sense and let the words look after themselves.

And this brings us at once to the root of the diction problem, namely, the undoubted difficulty which presents itself at times in reconciling the claims of good tone and clear enunciation. When a pupil is studying he practises upon the easiest vowel sounds and syllables which can be selected; and many singers, I am afraid, would like nothing better than to be allowed to continue singing upon these agreeable and grateful vocables to the end of their day.

Unfortunately, however, this is not quite possible, and so too many try to get over the difficulty by singing the words not in the way in which they should be pronounced, but in the manner most convenient to themselves. It is hardly necessary to say that this is all wrong and most inartistic, besides being quite unnecessary.

It may be said that it is easy for an Italian to speak thus, and it must certainly be agreed that we Italians are greatly favoured in having the most vocal and melodious of all languages to sing. With our open vowels we may be considered, indeed, to have every advantage in this respect, just as the Germans with their multiplicity of harsh and difficult and, to Italian ears, almost impossible consonants, have every disadvantage.

Yet the principle remains unaffected that every singer, in whatever language, who wishes to be considered a master of his art must contrive to reconcile the claims of good tone with those of accurate and intelligible diction, and the student cannot pay too much attention to this matter from the very moment that he begins to clothe his tones in words.

"Sing as you speak," is a saying which I have heard ascribed to that great master, Jean de Reszke, and though the advice cannot, perhaps, be taken quite literally, it certainly indicates the ideal to be kept in view. It is not feasible to obey the injunction quite literally because it is almost physically impossible to sing certain sounds on certain notes. On this account many teachers—Lamperti himself was one of them—sanction the deliberate modification of the proper vowel sounds or, preferably, the substitution of a more convenient word. But the object should certainly be to keep as near as may be practicable to the correct, natural pronunciation, whereas some seem to make it their aim almost to depart from this as far as possible.

One of the worst examples of execrable enunciation was given by one singer when giving an otherwise creditable rendering of Maude Valerie White's "Devout Lover." The words intended were "Burn at her altar," which were given "Burnateralter."

Some English singers have the habit of putting a vowel after a consonant, as in the word "Goodbye," which becomes "Goodabye" and which is absurd.

Baritones often have a habit of emphasising wrong words, of which one of the best examples is "Trumpeter, what *are* you sounding now?" Another absurdity.

One could multiply these examples indefinitely.

CHAPTER XX

LANGUAGE

"ITALIAN is the easiest language to sing, then comes Russian, and I should put English next. All languages affect the tone, unless the tone is first able to carry the weight of the language. A singer may study in any language, but in only one until after the tone is placed beyond any possibility of being affected by the demands of the different languages."

I am disposed to think that there is a good deal of truth in this. How serious is the influence exercised by the language used upon the quality of the tone produced is illustrated by German vocalism and American intonation. For here you have entire nations who, in the vocal sense, may be said to illustrate the evil effect upon tone of a harsh and nasal language.

German singing seems to be different, not merely in degree, but even in kind from that of other lands. In the case of even its best exponents there is a harshness and a tonelessness about it which differentiates it from that of any other race. German singers often have strong, lusty voices, likewise plenty of intelligence and dramatic feeling; but for beauty of tone and all the finer qualities of vocalism one listens for them in vain.

The fact is strange, but it can hardly be denied even by those least disposed to admit it. That one of the most musical nations in Europe should also be that of all others least dowered with the gift of song is a remarkable paradox which is not a little difficult to understand.

It is not a case of differences of taste. The point is that the German voice, as such, is indisputably inferior in point of quality to that of practically all the other European races. There is no discredit in the circumstance. It implies no reflection on anyone. It is merely an unfortunate physiological fact which must be accepted like any other of those decrees of Nature which are not to be gainsaid.

Such being the fact, how is it to be explained? Why is it that German singing is of this strange quality? How has it come about that so musical a race has been so shabbily treated by Nature in this important regard?

Various theories have been advanced. According to some the explanation is that it is the German language with its explosive consonants, harsh gutturals, and other unmelodious characteristics, which is at the bottom of the trouble.

Students of voice production will prove to you by ingenious experiments that the disposition of the vocal organs, breathing, and so forth, required for the utterance of the German language, are in themselves incompatible with the emission of a beautiful quality of vocal tone; and however this may be, it is hardly to be disputed that regarded from the standpoint of euphony, pure and simple, the German language is certainly not to be called melodious.

It seems quite a plausible theory, therefore, that harshness of language and harshness of voice are not disconnected, especially when the suggestion is fortified by the converse association of the most beautiful voices with the most mellifluous language, in the case of the Italians.

And if so much be admitted, it is obvious that it may indeed be a question of importance, as Signor Bonci has suggested, what language is employed by the student in that critical initial stage when his voice is being "placed."

For the rest it may be noticed that another great modern tenor, namely Caruso, insisted especially, when discussing this question of placing, upon the supreme necessity of freedom and ease and the absence of all unnecessary contractions of the muscles.

Signor Fucito tells us that on this point he expressed himself as follows: "It is necessary through

the aid of self-study and the help of a good singing teacher to become aware of every physical defect—such as contractions of the muscles of the
throat, of the face, or of the jaw—which can hin-
der the tone from being emitted in all its fullness
and purity. These rigid muscular contractions
bring about a throaty tone, which lacks support
and is incapable of purity and amplitude. . . .
The singer should apply himself to his study with
great naturalness and relaxation; this is the *sine
qua non* of beautiful cantilena singing."

With every word of these remarks I heartily
agree. Indeed, I imagine that they would gain the
universal assent of all qualified to write on the
subject.

The pronunciation of foreign languages is a
point to which the student can hardly give too
much attention. It also affords another argument
in favour of study abroad, since it is certain that
a foreign language cannot possibly be acquired so
effectually anywhere as in the land where it is
spoken. And foreign languages are indispensable
to a singer nowadays who aspires to be equal to all
the requirements of the modern répertoire.

True it may not be necessary to possess the
linguistic powers of a Mingotti, who spoke German, French, Italian, English, and Spanish. But
at least it may be laid down as an inexorable rule
that no one should ever attempt to sing in a foreign

tongue until he has acquired absolute command over every detail of its pronunciation by means of study, if not in the land itself, at any rate with a native.

Otherwise the result can only be a travesty of the composer's—or at all events of the poet's—intentions and a source of mirth to all hearers. Little do some artists realise, indeed, the impressions which they produce at times when, with misplaced assurance, they venture on songs in tongues with which they are imperfectly acquainted.

Even in the case of the best equipped it is a proceeding attended with risk to sing in a foreign language; but without complete knowledge there is no more certain way of exposing one's self to ridicule.

And I am afraid that it must be said that, contrary perhaps to the general belief, Italian suffers no less than any other language from misguided attempts of this kind. The idea is commonly entertained that Italian is "easy" to speak, but of course this is not the case if it is really to be properly spoken.

To which I may add that few peoples seem to experience more difficulty in mastering its subtleties than the English. It may be recalled, too, that this was also the view of Lamperti. Of all the European nations, he declared, the English, and especially Londoners, pronounced Italian worst.

The sounds that they produce, he remarked, are nearly all guttural, the vowels being excessively weak, while their accent was entirely wrong—the men, he added, being even worse than the women.

The Scotch, on the other hand, were not quite so bad in his judgment, while the Irish were best of all. Indeed, he agreed that the latter with study could learn to speak Italian quite wonderfully— as is illustrated, I may say, at the present time by Mr. John McCormack, who has a most admirable Italian diction. But it certainly is not often that one can speak in similar terms of the average English artist.

If anyone doubts this, let him read and ponder over some caustic remarks once made on this very point by the late Sir Charles Santley. Nothing was more deplorable, he said, than to hear the atrocious manner in which the beautiful Italian language was murdered at times by untrained English singers, and if, he added, they had any notion of the effect which they produced by such attempts upon such of their hearers as happened to be really familiar with the language, they would assuredly never make themselves so ridiculous again. Better a thousand times, he concluded, to sing all your life in your own tongue rather than make yourself a laughing-stock by attempting a task beyond your power.

To which I need hardly add that the same applies no less to French and German, though I am myself less qualified to speak concerning those languages.

It is not for me, perhaps, to say much about Wagner singing, which is so far removed from my own chosen province, but I may be permitted, perhaps, while on the subject of diction, to point to the appalling manner in which the divine art of singing has been perverted by Wagnerian singers under the mistaken notion that they were in this way carrying out the wishes of the sublime master.

I say "under the mistaken notion" because it is well known by those acquainted with the fact that the so-called "Bayreuth method" was as far removed as possible from Wagner's actual ideas. It is true that he attached the utmost importance to clear and emphatic enunciation of the words so that the course of the drama might be quite clearly understood, and therein he was quite right. But there is little reason to suppose that he was in reality satisfied with the actual results achieved by the German singers by whom his works were originally presented.

It is, indeed, an utter mistake to suppose that the harsh and strident singing of the average German vocalist was of a kind to commend itself to Wagner. On the contrary, it was one of his pet schemes, if I have not been misinformed, in connection with Bayreuth, to institute a School of

Singing which might lead to better things; and the kind of singing at which he aimed may be gathered from the fact that the teacher whom he wished to secure to carry out his views was none other than that famous exponent of Bel Canto, the late Señor Manuel García!

In the same connection, too, may be recalled the remark made by the composer after hearing a performance of "Lohengrin" (with the great Italian Wagnerian tenor Borgatti) on one occasion at Bologna. Almost for the first time, he said, he had heard his music really sung. All of which suggests how far they are from actually fulfilling the wishes of the master in continuing at Bayreuth the horrible vocal methods which had become so unfortunately associated with his name.

Chapter XXI

STYLE AND INTERPRETATION

D ICTION, it may be said, is included in Style;
but Style means a good deal more than
diction.

Style may be said, indeed, to mean everything
that the singer adds to the bare notes and directions of the printed page. These notes and directions are admittedly incomplete—a mere approxi-
mation to the composer's complete meaning. He
supplies in this way the bare facts with such additional hints as to expression and interpretation as
an imperfect system of notation allows. It is the
duty of his interpreters to supply what is missing
—to breathe the spirit of life into the dry bones
and to convert dead printed notes into living
human music.

To this end the singer must possess first of all
the requisite insight and understanding to grasp
the composer's purpose, next the personality and
magnetism to be able to realise it for his hearers,
and lastly the musical taste and knowledge required in order to present it in conformity with
the appropriate rules and traditions. In other

words, the singer must not merely sing the right notes, but sing them in the right way—with the right accent, the right phrasing, and in the right manner.

What is required may be best realised, perhaps, by comparing the delivery of a fine piece of poetry by a schoolgirl or schoolboy, say, with the delivery of the same lines by an accomplished actor or elocutionist. The words will be the same in both cases, but what a difference in the result! So in the case of music the notes sung will be the same whoever sings them, but the effect will be vastly different when they are sung by the trained artist.

Here it is that the student's general culture will bear fruit, in the imaginative insight and understanding, the good taste and the expression, which he brings to his task. And here, too, will his musical knowledge and intelligence be more particularly illustrated by the manner in which he conforms to the requirements of the particular kind of music which he is interpreting. For to do this aright a knowledge of the notes alone will not suffice.

He must be familiar also with the varying needs of the different schools of music, with the historical traditions associated with them, and so forth. Opera demands one kind of singing, oratorio another, German *Lieder* another, and so on through-

out; and each of these general classifications can
be subdivided in turn.

How different are the requirements of each is
best exemplified by the fact that so few succeed in
all. One singer will be great in opera, another in
oratorio, a third in *Lieder;* but only in the rarest
instances will you find one and the same artist ex-
celling in all. Why is this? Simply because their
respective requirements are so different.

For this reason the average artist will, I think,
usually be well advised to confine himself to the
class of work more particularly suited to his talent.
While it is well to cultivate versatility so far as
possible, it is a mistake to sing music of a kind for
which you are not suited. Patti loved Wagner, for
instance, and was a frequent visitor to Bayreuth.
But she did not sing his music. She liked to hear
it sung by others, but she realised that it was not
for her. Voice, personality, training, temperament, all impose necessary limitations.

People blame me sometimes, for instance, for
confining myself mainly to music of a certain
school. But I think I know best as to this, and
that I am exercising sound judgment in adopting
this course. There is much music which I admire
and love, but I do not always try to sing it. In
the same way I may admire frocks which I see on
other women, but I do not necessarily try to wear

the same myself. I have the good sense to recognise that they would not suit me.

Moreover, the field of music is so vast that to cultivate one or two departments thoroughly will be more than sufficient to tax the energy of the most ambitious. Make yourself master or mistress in your own chosen province, and you will have accomplished quite as much as any one need wish to.

And whatever style you cultivate get as near to perfection in it as you can possibly. Catalani said of Sontag: *"Elle est la première dans son genre; mais son genre n'est pas le premier."* This may or may not have been true. But Sontag was probably well pleased, in any case, to be *"la première."*

CHAPTER XXII

HOW I SING AN ARIA

TO sing a song or a big aria well you must, for
the time, be both the vocalist and composer
of the words and music you wish to express. If I
wish to sing, say, "Home Sweet Home," I must
imagine how far I am away from·sunny Italy, and
forget all the kindness and attention with which I
am surrounded here. Then, I begin to feel the
mood and homesickness coming to aid me, vocal
control must do the rest in making the song effective.

Or, again, if I wish to do justice to Sir Frederick
Cowen's charming little song, "The Swallows," I
must think of a lovely sunny morning and, mentally, "Open wide my lattice, letting in the laughing breeze," imagining all the joyous sense of life
that the arrival of the swallows brings to my naturally vivacious Southern nature.

Let us, however, take the Recitative and Polonaise from that brilliantly sparkling opera "Mignon," by Ambroise Thomas. First of all, I have to
study the setting of this great aria, and then study
the words, which, in English begin,

97

"Yes! for to-night I am Queen of the Fairies,
And here my golden sceptre see;
And behold these, my trophies!"

Yes; for to-night I am queen..... of.... the
fai-ries!   And here my gold-en scep-tre see;....
And be-hold   these my tro-phies

I ask myself what I might feel like were I able to become a fairy. Giving myself free rein, I sing the whole recitative much as I would speak it, only having in mind the notes, I attack them firmly, letting the conductor punctuate the whole with the accompaniment somewhat freely. In recitative, one must have fire and imagination, and, although reasonable attention must be paid to the valuation of notes—the full five beats, for example, on the long note of bars 6 and 7—it is the part of the accompanist to feel your pulse, as it were, and go with you. Now, on the same long note, be careful to carry a sense of increasing wonder, by making a *diminuendo,* then, with increasing verve, make a clean "turn" on beat four of the 8th bar, capped

by a triumphant pause, and, a clean interval of the
fifth with the word "trophies," on beats one and
two of bar 9.

Now we come to the actual Polacca, in which
tempo must be observed and all the tricks of brilliant vocal agility put into play. Remember, all
these "runs" and bravura passages must be clear—
every note like a fresh pea out of a pod or bullet
out of a machine gun! Observe the boldness of
"picking up" at the beginning of the polacca movement, and in bar 3 of this movement how smoothly
the detached notes have to be sung.

Here, again, there must be no scooping up an
octave, but a clear rise of the octave, giving the
sense of all, as it were, one piece. Thus, "I—I *am*
Titania," and repeat the same words with even
greater fervour, treating all the words and music
with the same mentality and as vital to the whole.

Many so-called intellectual singers prefer *Lieder,*
because they cannot vocalise the fine, dashing,
graceful runs of florid music, not because of its lack
of intellectual requirements. What could better
express the vivacious joy of a fairy queen than the

triplet passages on the exclamation *"Ah!"* bars
14 and 15 of the polacca movement.

When we come to bars 29 and 30, there is the
chance of a lifetime with the cadenza-like string of

ry! Ah!..

fifteen notes, in the neatest sets of three, and they
should be as perfect as though played by Kreisler
on the violin.

Later on we come to some roulade passages of
six notes on the same exclamation "Ah!" (bars 43,
44, and 45) which must be sung with increasing
verve, so that the wood wind of the orchestra

fai - - ry! Ah!..

comes running up perfectly in tune and tempo, as
it were from right under your last note. Here,
much depends upon the cue of the conductor, but,
changing one's manner and keeping up the growing
joyfulness, you begin a new era, as it were, with

the words, "Bright troops of fairies hover round
me." Thus, the aria works on, until, on the last
beat of bar 54 and bar 55 there is a suggestion of

a fairy call. A dream-like waltz, in wide contrast,
follows. Unless one feels this, the brilliance we
have worked up is losing the value of contrast with

this shimmer, as it were, of gleaming moonlight.
On this breaks the brilliant passages of the flute,
which may be the task of some fairy worker in the

real fairyland! I must be wafted along in smooth
subservience to the brilliance of the accompaniment for the next few bars, until I repeat the

lovely melody at bar 62 when I begin to add—as
scored in the part—some grace notes and florid
passages, and gradually awaken until, at bar 79, I
have ascended to a full top B, preceded by a "trill"
or "shake," that leads up to the brilliant burst of
the orchestra back to the polacca-like movement,
and to the finale. This must be one increasing
triumph, over the much-talked-of top E flat, the
roulades, grace notes, trills, and cadenza-like pas-

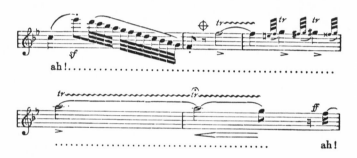

sages for sheer *joie de vivre*. Yet all this depends
upon how well you have conditioned yourself,
practised those tiring vowel sounds, scales, sustained passages, to which I commend you before
essaying the brilliant Polonaise from "Mignon"
that has given me many triumphs, yet still calls for
all I can give, as it will to the end of the chapter.

Chapter XXIII

PRACTISING

IS it necessary to say that daily practice is indispensable to the student—as it is also to the finished artist? A celebrated violinist used to say, "If I cease practising for one day I know it when I next play; if for two days my enemies know it; if for three the public know it." It is the same with the voice, although some voices, no doubt, require less daily exercising than others.

Some fortunate ones, indeed, have been able to dispense with it almost entirely. On the day of a performance the great Chaliapine warms his voice up for a period of thirty or forty minutes only. On other days and when on vacation he rarely practises, except for getting up new music, and even this is more of a mental process. It is said of Mario also that at the height of his fame he never practised more than ten minutes a day, and that just before he was leaving for the Opera House, while his servant would be standing, watch in hand, assuring him that he would be late for the performance if he did not start at once. But that, of course, was an exceptional case.

On the other hand, Battistini is most lavish with his practising and rarely a day passes that he does not put in one or two hours of solid singing. This no doubt accounts for the extraordinary command he has over tone, phrasing and breathing. There is great truth in the saying that practice makes perfect, but how many of us have the robust and natural organ that Battistini is blessed with. I always thought that the reason of this was the fact that Battistini, who could well have trained as a tenor, elected to become a baritone, thus evading the strain of forcing high "C's" out of his voice.

At the same time even practising should not be carried to excess. Many singers have, indeed, often done their voices great harm by practising too much. The vocal cords are exceedingly delicate and cannot be used too carefully. There can be no doubt that the wonderful preservation of Patti's voice was due in large measure to the extraordinary prudence and care with which she husbanded it. By never singing at rehearsals, by never singing when she was in the least degree out of health or tired, and so on, she added years probably to the length of her career. And all singers should act as far as possible on the same principle.

There should never be the smallest strain in practising, for instance. For this reason it is advisable to practise with the half voice mostly and

only rarely at the extremities of the compass—
and then with great care and discretion. In the
same way there should never be any sense of fatigue, still less of hoarseness, after practice.

It is, indeed, in the ordinary way a sure sign that
something is wrong, either with your vocal organs
or with your methods, if this occurs often, and the
matter should be investigated accordingly—even
to the extent of changing your teacher if necessary.

If, however, the trouble is only temporary, a
brief suspension of exercising may be all that is
necessary. But in this case be careful not to re-
sume your practising until the trouble has completely disappeared. Far better drop your practising for a week, or a month, if necessary, than
attempt to sing when your organs are not in perfect order.

That is to say, if there is really definite trouble.
If, on the other hand, it is merely a little hoarseness, such as many singers are subject to, then
judicious exercising—please notice that I empha-
sise judicious—may be the best thing for it. This
is, however, essentially a matter upon which you
must be guided by your teacher—or even if necessary by a doctor.

Madame Lilli Lehmann prescribes, for instance,
what she calls the Great Scale as an invaluable

remedy for all manner of vocal ills—meaning simply long slow scales of sustained notes steadily repeated. Here is what she said, for instance, on this point:

"The great scale properly employed in practice accomplishes wonders. It equalises the voice, makes it flexible and noble, gives strength to all weak places, operates to repair all breaks and faults that exist, and controls the voice to the very heart. Nothing escapes it. It is the Guardian Angel of the voice. I sing it every day, often twice, even if I have to sing one of my greatest rôles in the evening. I can rely absolutely on its assistance."

And, as I have said, she prescribed this very exercise not only for daily practice when one is well, but also as a remedy for troubles when the voice is out of order. I may be permitted, perhaps, to quote in this connection another interesting passage:

"I myself had to sing 'Norma' in Vienna some years ago and got up in the morning quite hoarse. By nine o'clock I tried my invaluable remedy, but could not sing above A flat, although in the evening I should have to reach high D flat and E flat. I was on the point of giving up because the case seemed to be so desperate. Nevertheless, I practised till 11 o'clock, half an hour at a time, and noticed that I was gradually getting better. In the evening I had my D flat and E flat at my command so that people said they had seldom heard me sing so well."

I have quoted this advice of Lilli Lehmann because it is of interest and value as coming from so great an authority, but I do not wish it to be understood that this has been my own precise practice, for this is not the case. But as to the general value of scales for practising purposes there is, of course, no possible doubt. Scales are, indeed, the foundation of all useful practice, especially at first.

Marchesi, for instance, relied on them almost exclusively in the earlier stages—long sustained tones, repeated again and again until her fastidious ear was satisfied; and no pupil can possibly fail to benefit from such exercise. Even for the acquisition of velocity, as I have said elsewhere, scales—and quite slow ones at first—are indispensable.

Of more elaborate exercises there are none better, so far as I know, than those to be found in Concone, while for advanced pupils well-chosen numbers from the great Italian operatic masters, Rossini, Donizetti, Bellini, and the rest, can be utilised with great advantage. This includes mezzo-sopranos, contraltos, as well as sopranos. My maestro would make them all sing "Una voce poco fa" transposed, saying that it was a vocal massage.

But it is rather a matter for the individual teacher to prescribe what is required in this way, since all voices will not need the same.

As to the period and duration of practising, my own plan is to practise twice a day—at ten in the morning for an hour, with intervals of rest; and again in the afternoon, before dinner, for the same time.   But the beginner should not practise for more than ten or fifteen minutes at a time, and should leave off immediately his voice begins to feel tired.

To which, I would add, that it is of the utmost importance not only what one practises but *how*. Ten minutes' practice with the maximum of thought and concentration will be of more value than a whole hour of mere mechanical scales and arpeggi, sung without thought and care.

The pupil, while practising, should listen to himself with the utmost vigilance all the time—criticising ruthlessly every tone, and seeking always to eradicate every fault and blemish.   It is for lack of this *mental* effort that pupils so often practise in vain—improving themselves in certain respects perhaps, but never acquiring that beauty of tone and perfection of execution which should be the foundation of all.

I would repeat here, indeed, what I have said before, that unsparing self-criticism is the root of all progress. Nor should this ever cease. As a great artist remarked in some words which I quoted earlier, the true artist will continue studying and practising and improving to the end of his day.

Read, for instance, what Signor Fucito tells us of Caruso:

"No one could have been a severer critic of Caruso's art than Caruso himself. He worked with tremendous concentration, and his acute ear was ever ready to descry the slightest flaw in the tone production, in quality or the interpretation of a musical passage."

And again:

"There were times when he refused to rest, singing a passage or phrase over and over again, each time with another vocal modulation of colouring until he got the expression and quality that satisfied his exacting musical taste."

It is interesting to note, by the way, that Caruso practised always, or nearly always, with the full voice—a procedure which is not, however, as I have already said, to be generally recommended.

Incidentally in practising the student should avoid the acquisition of bad habits of standing, undesirable movements with the hands, and so on, and should also keep careful check upon his facial expressions. For the latter purpose it is an excellent plan to practise before a mirror, since this is the surest way to avoid the unconscious cultivation of undesirable tricks which, once they have been acquired, may prove most difficult to get rid of.

In the case of operatic artists it is a good plan also to practise in costume in order to become accustomed to the dress which one will be wearing in the actual performance, and thus to avoid any sense of awkwardness which may be otherwise experienced. And for the same reason when any particular number has to be sung in any special manner from the physical point of view, as, for instance, sitting down, or kneeling, it is well to become accustomed to this also beforehand.

CHAPTER XXIV

THE ARTIST AND THE GRAMOPHONE

BEFORE leaving the subject of practising I should like to add a word as to the value of the gramophone to the intelligent student. This is, indeed, a truly invaluable adjunct. If to hear the greatest singers is the finest of all experiences for the student, how can it indeed be otherwise? For here in the most convenient manner possible is the means provided for doing this. In the earlier pages of this volume I have recorded what inestimable advantages I derived in my own case from the constant hearing of fine singing from my earliest childhood. Now, by means of the gramophone, the same advantage is at the command of every one wheresoever he, or she, may happen to reside.

In my younger days only those dwelling in the great capitals could hope to hear such artists as Patti, Tamagno, Caruso, Battistini, and so forth, and even those only if means permitted, which was not often in the case of poor students.

To-day any one can enjoy this priceless privilege, wherever he may happen to reside, for a comparatively small outlay through the agency of the gramophone.

And he can hear them not only now and again, but as often as ever he likes and by his own fireside. If he happens to be studying some particular rôle he can be "coached" in this most practical and unrivalled manner by all the greatest artists of the day. He can take a particular aria and hear it sung by Caruso again and again until he is familiar with every detail of his rendering—can note his breathing, his phrasing, and every other detail in a manner which would be quite impossible by any other means.

And having heard Caruso he can then hear the same number sung by various other great artists if he chooses, and benefit still more by comparing their respective readings—by noting how they resemble one another or how they differ, as the case may be, incidentally learning in the process how widely one interpretation may differ from another and still be of the highest order.

Not only this, but he can familiarise himself with entire operas in the same way, for certain of the companies issue complete albums of the best known works which are reproduced in their entirety— vocal parts, orchestra, and all in this marvellous manner. One would think, indeed, that the coming generation should provide us with fine singers in such plenty as the world has never known before with the aid of such priceless help.

Whether it will be so or not remains to be seen. But certainly it may be said that never before have students been so wonderfully helped. I myself have pleasure in testifying that I have derived the greatest benefit as well as delight from the records of Patti, while Mr. John McCormack has similarly acknowledged his indebtedness to the wonderful renderings of Caruso.

And I hope in all modesty that students of the present generation may derive similar help in turn from the records which I myself have made. Beyond a doubt the gramophone should be the guide, philosopher, and friend—the most trusted and most competent aid and coadjutor—not only to every student, but also to every teacher of the present day.

Of course, the pupil is only human and often reluctant to believe that there are grave faults in his voice. Whilst others can detect his mistakes, the pupil cannot listen intelligently to his own faulty emission while singing.

But take him to a recording-room and get him to sing into the recording-horn, and let him listen as the operator tries over the record he has made. He is sure to be surprised to find how many faults there are.

His production may be throaty, nasal, or what you will. It is all brought out clearly by the gramophone.

There is no instrument that is so calculated to remove the conceit from a young artist as the gramophone. To watch his face as he first listens to his own voice is usually to enjoy a miniature pantomime.

Nevertheless, the gramophone is a spur to drive the artist forward to perfection, and, of course, a great aid to the music professor.

CHAPTER XXV

STUDYING A RÔLE

DIFFERENT artists have different methods of studying their parts, but all I think will be agreed on one point, namely, that they cannot possibly be learned too thoroughly. Marvellous stories are told, no doubt, of difficult rôles having been completely mastered by prodigious efforts in a fabulously short time. But he is taking terrible risks who attempts a *tour de force* of this kind, and in my own opinion no artist should ever be asked to do this. To master a rôle in the proper way should be a matter of weeks and months, not to say years, of careful study so that it becomes part and parcel, as it were, of the very being of the artist. Then, and then only, can it be attempted on the stage with that absolute confidence and assurance and that entire freedom from anxiety without which the best results cannot possibly be hoped for.

Very foolish, or at all events very courageous, is the young artist who for the sake of an appearance at all costs essays a part which he, or she, has not thoroughly prepared beforehand—for that way

115

disaster lies. A part simply cannot be too well studied if failure and mishaps are to be absolutely assured against.

Let it be remembered especially by the student who runs through a part so easily in the privacy of his study with the aid of a friendly accompanist at the piano, how infinitely more difficult are the conditions on the actual stage—alike in the psychological and purely material senses.

There is the consciousness, in the first place, of being part now of a huge inexorable organisation which admits of no error or failure under any circumstances, and that at first has an almost paralysing effect upon the faculties. There is the consciousness of that eager, critical public on the other side of the footlights and of all that there is at stake should any failure occur. There is the difficulty in the physical sense of hearing the orchestra properly, which seems so far off and so infinitely less helpful than the friendly homely piano. There are the perturbing factors of one's costume, action, business. In short, the whole thing is utterly different, and for this reason, therefore, the young artist cannot be too firmly grounded in his rôle if he is to be proof against all the possibilities of failure and all mischances and mishaps in the hour of trial.

As to the actual process of mastering a rôle I believe thoroughly in the practice of studying it at the outset apart from the music. Read the whole book through and master the story and the drama completely in the first instance. Get every twist and turn and every detail of it into your mind. Try to visualise and represent it to yourself as realistically as possible.

Imagine that it all actually occurred and that you were, in fact, the character whose part you are to represent. Learn all you can about the period of the story, the scene of the action, the circumstances of the time, and so on, so as to realise it all as vividly as possible.

And then, having done this, study with equal thoroughness every detail of your own part. It may be only a small one. Never mind. You can make it just as lifelike and as perfect in its way as one of more importance if you make the most of it.

It was in this way that Mario always studied his parts, and most other great artists, I think, will be found to adopt a similar method. We read of Mario that no trouble was too great and no research too laborious to ensure that any rôle which he had undertaken should be represented as correctly and as perfectly as possible. Nor did his fastidious care end there, for he paid the greatest attention to his words also and even rewrote every line of his part in Gounod's "Faust" because the words of the original Italian version were not sufficiently singable to please him.

It was Mario, also, who said that unless he had all that he was singing about in his head as well as in his throat he could never hope to do justice to his part.

It is the old, old story. The greatest results in anything are only to be obtained by unsparing labour. It may not be a complete statement of the case to say that genius is only an infinite capacity for taking pains. But it is certainly true to say that that capacity is almost always associated with the highest genius. Caruso supplied a more recent instance. He took endless pains to get his parts right in every detail. He was as careful, we read, about creating the proper make-up for the character which he was impersonating as he was about studying the proper gestures, declamation, and musical expression.

Signor Fucito writes:

"He pondered the mental, emotional and moral traits of the character as they were revealed not only in his own lines and music, but throughout the entire opera. If he found that insufficient he searched elsewhere—in art, in literature, in history. When he was preparing the rôle of Samson he went to the Bible for additional enlightenment on that legendary hero in order that he might visualise him more vividly; and when he was studying Eleazar he sought advice on Jewish customs from a prominent Yiddish actor of New York."

Respecting "make-up" this should be done as carefully and artistically as possible, bearing in mind always that although some of the audience may be a long way off, others will be much nearer, while opera glasses will further help to abridge the distance and to reveal every detail.

CHAPTER XXVI

CHOICE OF DÉBUT WORK

AS regards the choice of opera for début purposes I need hardly say that this is a matter of great importance which should be most carefully considered. If you happen to be exceptionally gifted and possess the advantage of powerful connections you may perhaps be able to appear at once in a rôle of the first importance, but my opinion is that it is usually much better to begin with smaller parts and acquire the necessary stage experience before attempting one of the more exacting rôles.

You may, of course, have such natural gifts and be so well trained and coached for the purpose that you may achieve success at a bound, but the chances are against this, and it is much more likely that you will fall short of your expectations and thereby imperil your career at the outset by making a false start. *C'est le premier pas,* etc., and it is much better to begin modestly and learn your business thoroughly before attempting the higher flights. Then when you are properly qualified and have acquired the necessary experience you can take a more important part with the assurance that you will be able at least to do full justice to yourself and to make the utmost of your natural powers.

There is another reason, too, why it is a mistake, as a rule, to attempt the heavier rôles too soon—namely, the fact that the voice and the general physique, apart from the question of training and experience, are seldom ready for these at first. I have, indeed, known more than one case in which a career of promise has been ruined after a brilliant start by subjecting a young singer too soon to the heavy strain of the most important parts.

Study these rôles by all means and have them ready—or one or two of them—in case some exceptional or unexpected opportunity should present itself. But do not be in too great a hurry to appear in them. It is a much safer course, as a rule, to make good at first in those of a less ambitious kind; and you need never be afraid that good work in these will go unnoticed or unrewarded. But whichever part you choose for the purpose it should naturally be one which is well suited to your capacity and in which you are confident of being able to do your best.

If the novice can attach himself or herself to some provincial opera company at a nominal salary for the purpose of training and experience, this is often a good plan. In Italy almost every provincial city has a small season of opera, and impresarios in most cases are ready to give a promising singer a début without pay in order to reduce their expenses. But in some instances if a singer desires to make a début in a certain rôle and imposes this on the impresario she will be required to help to finance the opera by the payment of a few thousand lire. This is often done, but in some instances with sad results, because it is usually an indifferent artist who forces a début in this way, often against the better judgment of the manager.

I have known instances, indeed, where a singer has obtained a début on these terms, and the audience, after hearing the singer, has protested so vigorously that the unfortunate novice has had to be withdrawn in favour of a more satisfactory substitute in order to pacify the public.

In one instance I remember a Canadian tenor of tremendous size, but with a voice more like a mad bull's than that of a human being, who thought he would make an ideal Othello. He was wealthy and paid the management 25,000 lire for a début. After the first act such a commotion was created in the theatre that the carabinieri had to step in and decide that either the show should be stopped or else continued by another artist.

Shortly afterwards columns appeared in the American papers about the harsh treatment of foreign singers in Italy. I can only say, however, that in my judgment it is utterly wrong to force on the public artists who are manifestly incapable, and that in this particular case the punishment fitted the crime!

In cases where there really are voice and merit such methods should be quite unnecessary, since managers are only too eager to secure fresh talent and to offer suitable opportunities for appearing before the public to those who possess it.

Just another suggestion. Don't be induced to accept a dramatic rôle if your voice is purely lyric. Don't even be tempted. Certain *maestri* are always looking for voices that can be heard above their orchestras. They never find one, because it doesn't exist; but the path of their search is strewn with wrecked voices.

CHAPTER XXVII

REHEARSALS

R EHEARSALS are a necessary evil and the sensible artist will try to make the best of them. Undoubtedly they are very tedious and trying, but they are quite unavoidable unless you happen to have attained sufficient eminence to be dispensed attendance at them. And even then it is not always wise to avoid them if you wish to procure the best results.

Patti, throughout the greater part of her career, never attended any rehearsals. But then she always sang in the best-known operas with thoroughly experienced fellow-artists who were carefully instructed as to her requirements. But it is hardly necessary to say that her case was exceptional.

Some artists are very trying at rehearsals by coming with their parts imperfectly prepared, by arriving late, and so on, and in such cases the company in general is fortunate if the manager is sufficiently firm to insist on proper discipline being observed.

A strict conductor who allows no trifling of this

kind is, indeed, the truest friend of the artists, and his authority should be recognised accordingly by one and all. It is of the utmost importance that artists should be thoroughly acquainted with their parts, and they should take advantage of rehearsals to master every detail of their action, business, and so on, leaving absolutely nothing to chance.

There is, however, no need to sing with full voice at rehearsals; indeed, this is not desirable. But one should naturally sing loud enough to indicate quite clearly one's intentions. Nor should the inexperienced artist show any reluctance to take advice from the stage manager when it is given. For his judgment will probably be better than yours, and in any case it is your business to do as he directs.

Chapter XXVIII

CONTRACTS

IN the case of young singers with very promising voices, impresarios are often found who are willing to finance the period of instruction for a term of say five years. Their calculations are that in the last few years of this period the artist will become a profitable investment for them.

In the case of a poor artist this is often a very good plan, since it is to the interest of the impresario to assist in making a name and a position for the artist as well as in seeing that he has a proper training. And the latter may easily find himself the gainer by the arrangement therefore.

Speaking generally, however, I am not very much in favour of such contracts, for the simple reason that, the career of an artist being so short, he ought not to be placed in the position of expending his powers for the benefit of another person. I have known artists drawing £100 a performance who were receiving a mere £10 a week under such an agreement as I have described; and this is, of course, a very unsatisfactory and even heartbreaking state of things.

Caruso was one, it will be remembered, who entered into such a contract as a student which, however, he finally succeeded in getting rescinded, though not before he had had recourse to the law courts for this purpose.

As to contracts made later, when a proper position has been secured, the artist will not usually need much advice regarding these, since he is generally quite able to look after himself. "Too well, indeed," it is sometimes said, by directors and managers.

Yet it must be remembered that, as noted above, the vocalist's career is usually very brief. The years of gain may be from five to twenty, but are rarely much more than ten. I have known great artists who have lasted for but a few seasons. On the other hand, I can recall some like Battistini who have had over forty years of lucrative employment. But this is very rare.

Are they not justified, therefore, in requiring generous payment while they can obtain it? Also it must be remembered that great singers are exceptionally endowed, and as such are entitled to demand exceptional rewards. In which connection one may recall the famous reply of the dancer Gabrielli to the Empress Catherine of Russia. The Empress was staggered by the terms which she demanded and declared that not even her Field-Marshals received so much. Whereupon

Gabrielli recommended the Empress to get her Marshals to dance for her.

Some of the most exacting contracts ever made by a singer were, I suppose, those of Catalani. In her agreements when she was singing in London she used to stipulate for half of the receipts throughout the entire season, while she inserted further such conditions as the following: "Madame Catalani shall choose and direct the operas which she is to sing; she shall likewise have the choice of the performers in them; and she will have no orders to receive from anyone."

Madame Patti in turn received as much as £1000 a performance from Mapleson in America. But then Patti was—Patti! Most artists are content with less! And to such I would say as my final word on this point: "Do not forget during the days of your necessarily brief prosperity to make provision at all costs for the future."

Chapter XXIX

CONCERT WORK

IF I have spoken largely about opera in these pages, this is because with my experience it comes most naturally to me to do this. But concert work—of which also I have done my share— is of course equally important, and a few words on this subject, therefore, may not come amiss.

It is hardly necessary to say that the kind of singing which is suitable for the stage is not always equally in keeping on the platform. It is the difference here between acting and recitation.

On the stage you are actually impersonating the character you represent, and the fullest amount of realism is therefore permissible—indeed, essential. On the platform the same amount of licence is not allowable. You are here not impersonating, but interpreting at one remove, so to speak.

You are not pretending to represent the actual character of the song; you are reproducing in *your own personality* the feelings and emotions involved. Or as one might put it, the art of the stage is representative; that of the concert platform is reproductive.

All this must be borne in mind, therefore, by the artist who turns from the stage to the concert room. The effect produced may be just as great, but it must be achieved in a different way—without action, without gesture even, but with the maximum of intensity none the less—secured by means of the voice, the expressiveness of the singing and the personality and temperament of the singer alone.

And these will be all-sufficient for those who know their business; nor should they be exceeded in the ordinary way. Yet if it comes naturally to you to go a little further now and again, I do not know that it need be condemned.

Observe, however, that I say "if it comes naturally to you." Otherwise, it will be forced and theatrical and will certainly not achieve its purpose. It is purely a question of temperament. Be natural and spontaneous and you will not go far astray. Northern peoples indulge sparingly in gestures on the concert platform, but yet get great results without their aid.

We Latin races are less restrained in this respect because this is in accordance with our natural temperaments. It is the difference between one who gesticulates freely in ordinary speech and one who never stirs a finger. One would not counsel the Englishman to copy the foreigner's gestures for it would not come naturally to him to do this; but

one would not have a Frenchman or an Italian
without them.

And so it is in singing. If an occasional gesture
comes naturally to you there is no need to repress
it, even if you cannot be recommended to go as far
in this respect in the concert room as Jenny Lind
did on one occasion if report may be trusted. It
is recorded that once when singing Agathe's prayer
from "Der Freischütz" at a concert at Norwich
she was so carried away that she actually fell on
her knees on the platform and so finished the air!
That was, perhaps, overdoing things. Certainly I
have never heard of even an Italian concert-singer
going quite so far.

I need hardly add, while on the subject of concert deportment, that a pleasing and ingratiating
manner is also much to be desired, though this is a
matter that seems to be strangely overlooked too
often by young artists of the present day. One
might think almost from the manners of some of
them that they consider themselves to be confer-
ring the greatest possible favour upon their hearers
by condescending to sing to them.

And doubtless in many cases they actually do
think this! But they should endeavour not to indicate the fact quite so clearly by their demeanour.
I have seen artists of this self-sufficient type who
actually make not the slightest response, or barely
any, when an audience is good enough to applaud

them! This sort of thing is quite incomprehensible to me, and I am sure that if those who behave thus had any conception of the impression which they produce they would speedily mend their manners.

CHAPTER XXX

HEALTH, DIET, ETC.

GOOD health is essential to a singer, and it must be most carefully preserved. To this end you should live as wholesome and regular an existence as possible, seeing that you get plenty of fresh air and taking such exercise as may be found convenient, but without overdoing things in the latter respect, since undue muscular exertion is sometimes prejudicial.

Moderation in diet is also advisable, avoiding especially all highly seasoned dishes, pepper, pickles, and the like, and in the matter of alcohol, if this be taken, confining one's self to the lightest kinds of wines.

As for smoking I prohibit it entirely, as I consider it to be the greatest enemy of the vocal cords, although I am well aware, of course, that some of the most famous singers have been inveterate smokers.

Of Mario, for instance, we are told that he was never seen without a cigar in his mouth except when he was eating. He smoked, it is recorded, even in his bath, although it may be noted that

even he expressly avoided cigarettes, confining himself exclusively to cigars.

Caruso, again, was another tremendous smoker,
and I suppose there are few male vocalists, at any
rate, who deny themselves in this respect entirely.
But I have no doubt that it would be better for
their vocal organs if they did so all the same.

Coughs and colds are, of course, the greatest
bugbear of the singer, and to assist in securing im-
munity from these do not allow your throat to become too sensitive by wrapping up too much.
Bathing the throat with cold water helps also to-
wards this end. When overheated and perspiring
never delay changing into dry clothes and be especially careful always to keep the feet dry.

Yet with all the precautions in the world the
time will come when concerts or performances
must be given under unfavourable conditions, and
in these circumstances the art and the courage of
the singer alone will carry her through.

Often I have undertaken a concert rather than
disappoint the public when suffering from a bad
cold. But I have been able by will power to do
wonders in these circumstances, and more often
than not I have been rewarded by a Press which
said that I had never sung better.

I have known Caruso, under such circumstances,
the morning before a widely advertised concert, at
which an audience of perhaps 10,000 people was

likely to be present, to wake up and find himself entirely without voice.

In the instance I have in mind he telegraphed for a celebrated throat specialist in New York to come immediately to Pittsburg, where just previous to the concert he underwent heroic treatment. This meant the administering of a stimulant to the vocal cords which contracted them for a period of a few hours.

Thereby he was enabled to fulfil his engagement, though the after-results put him out of action for at least a week.

A singer cannot hope always to be absolutely at his best, and this fact should be realised from the first by young artists. Frequently, prior to a performance, if the artist cannot bring off certain customary effects he, or she, will be thrown immediately into a state of distraction and despair. This, however, is all wrong.

Engagements must be kept, and more often than not, as I have suggested, the artist will find when the time comes that his apprehension has been quite uncalled for. Strung up by the needs of the case, and making a special call upon all his resources, mental and emotional as well as merely vocal, he will very likely do even better than usual.

He should bear this in mind, therefore, another time, and never lose his head even though he may think that he has lost his voice!

At the same time this is not to say that really serious voice trouble should be ignored, and I myself make it a practice in every large town where I am accustomed to stay for any length of time to learn of a suitable medical man or voice specialist to whom I can repair for advice in case of need.

As to one's régime on the day when one is actually singing this merits a few words perhaps. Having gone to bed betimes the day before, so as to secure a long night of unbroken rest, I myself do not usually rise until about ten or eleven, when I have a light breakfast of tea and toast and soft-boiled eggs. For lunch, if one may call it such, after a short walk, I have merely a cup of cocoa and a little fruit, and nothing more until after the concert. Most other artists of my acquaintance do likewise.